PRAISE FOR
The Cleansing
Power of the Blood

Dr. Sandra Kennedy is a wonderful woman of God whom my wife and I have known and respected for many years. I thoroughly enjoyed reading her book on the Blood of Jesus, and I highly recommend it to anyone who is interested in living in victory every day—and not just on Sunday! When you start drawing on the power of the blood regularly, you are going to see change in yourself, your circumstances, and even in the lives of your loved ones. This is an excellent book, and I hope you enjoy it as much as I did.

—Dr. Jesse Duplantis
Jesse Duplantis Ministries
Hammond, Louisiana

Are you willing to think "out of the box"—even about the blood of Jesus? Sandra Kennedy is! She offers an exciting and challenging understanding of the efficacy of the blood of Jesus. All believers rest in the efficacy of the blood of Jesus for salvation yet fail to apply it to unconquered areas in their personal lives. Dr. Kennedy stresses that as believer priests we may also use this authority to apply the blood over the lives of our family and wayward loved ones. This is worth the read!

—Dr. Iverna M. Tompkins
Iverna Tompkins Ministries
Scottsdale, Arizona

I am delighted to write this for my admired friend and colleague, Dr. Sandra Kennedy. As I read this book, I could hear this anointed servant–teacher pouring out her own heart to her beloved flock. She is a passionate and transparent seeker after God. Her heart is pure and fixed on Jesus, and it shows in this book. *The Cleansing, Healing Power of the Blood* is a plea for God's people to not only experience the cleansing work of the Spirit but also to exercise their priesthood in helping others to a life of forgiveness and power. I heartily recommend this book to preachers, teachers, leaders, and all who seek a deeper experience of Christ and His love.

—DR. RONALD E. COTTLE
Founder, Embassy School of Leadership
Founder and President Emeritus, Christian Life School
of Theology (CLST Global)

The
Cleansing, Healing
Power *of The*
BLOOD

DESTINY IMAGE BOOKS BY DR. SANDRA KENNEDY

Preparations for a Move of God in Your Life

The Simplicity of Healing

The Cleansing, Healing Power of the Blood

The
Cleansing, Healing
Power *of The*
BLOOD

DR. SANDRA G. KENNEDY

© Copyright 2018 – Dr. Sandra G. Kennedy

All rights reserved. This book is protected by the copyright laws of the United States of America. This book may not be copied or reprinted for commercial gain or profit. The use of short quotations or occasional page copying for personal or group study is permitted and encouraged. Permission will be granted upon request. Unless otherwise identified, Scripture quotations are taken from the New King James Version®. Copyright © 1982 by Thomas Nelson. Used by permission. All rights reserved. Scripture quotations marked KJV are from the King James version of the Bible. Scripture quotations marked (NLT) are taken from the Holy Bible, New Living Translation, copyright © 1996, 2004, 2007, 2013, 2015 by Tyndale House Foundation. Used by permission of Tyndale House Publishers, Inc., Carol Stream, Illinois 60188. All rights reserved. All emphasis within Scripture quotations is the author's own. Word definitions are derived from Strong's Exhaustive Concordance of the Bible, Nashville, TN: Thomas Nelson Publishers, 1997. Please note that the name satan and related names are not capitalized. We choose not to acknowledge him, even to the point of violating grammatical rules.

DESTINY IMAGE® PUBLISHERS, INC.

P.O. Box 310, Shippensburg, PA 17257-0310

"Promoting Inspired Lives."

This book and all other Destiny Image and Destiny Image Fiction books are available at Christian bookstores and distributors worldwide.

For more information on foreign distributors, call 717-532-3040.

Or reach us on the Internet: www.destinyimage.com

Cover design by: Eileen Rockwell
Interior design by Terry Clifton

ISBN 13 TP: 978-0-7684-1939-9
ISBN 13 EBook: 978-0-7684-1940-5
ISBN HC: 978-0-7684-1942-9
ISBN LP: 978-0-7684-1941-2

Previously published as *Hope for the Heart* by Creation House, Strang Company, 2007; ISBN: 978-1-59979-159-3

For Worldwide Distribution, Printed in the U.S.A.
2 3 4 5 6 / 21 20 19 18

This book is dedicated to all the wonderful people, especially those in my church, who have taken the teachings on the cleansing power of the blood to heart, applied them to their lives, and have seen tremendous victory. And to all who encouraged me to put the teachings in writing so that others may discover the cleansing power of the Blood of Jesus, know how to release that power in their lives, and walk in victory.

ACKNOWLEDGMENTS

I would like to offer a special word of appreciation to Reverend John Stocker whose teachings over the years have given me great inspiration.

My sincerest thanks to Charlene Kiraly, Reverend Velda Schirhart, Lynette Whitlock, and Dr. Robin O'Neal whose dedication and efforts have helped make this book a reality.

CONTENTS

FOREWORD

Dr. Sandra Kennedy is a wonderful woman of God whom my wife and I have known and respected for many years. She has the unique ability to put you at ease, make you feel welcome, and share the Word in a real and easy-to-understand way. On top of that, the woman just flat-out makes me smile! This book comes from her heart and her perspective as a psychologist, therapist, counselor, and anointed minister of the Gospel, and it will show you a different side of the blood of Jesus—one that reaches beyond the sinner's prayer and into the everyday, ongoing life of the believer.

Sandra's book addresses some of the issues we all deal with from time to time. It is filled with the Word, her wisdom, and her wonderful personality. I highly recommend it to anyone who is interested in living in victory every day—not just on Sunday! I believe that, when you start drawing on the power of the Blood regularly, you are going to see change in yourself, your circumstances, and even in the lives of your loved ones.

Whether you have been saved five minutes or fifty years, you are going to learn something from this book. I did, and I enjoyed every minute of it. The Blood of Jesus is what gives every one of us hope for today, tomorrow, and the far-off future. The Blood *never* loses its power—it remains a continual source of grace, mercy, and power that we can draw upon and see results. The Blood cleans up our mind. It cleans up our body. It cleans up situations that we don't know what to do about! The Blood *is* power; and in this book, you will learn how to use it in a way you may never have thought of before. Sandra has some great revelation about the ongoing cleansing power of the Blood that is going to lift your heart and make your journey in this life easier and a lot more joyful.

So, sit down, get comfortable, and get ready to start seeing yourself through the powerful, precious, and finished work of the Blood. You are going to learn how to stop trying to become what you already are—free—and start living the good life that Jesus came to give to you. As she would say, it is time to start flying with the eagles and stop crash-landing with the turkeys!

Are you ready to learn something new? Good! This is a book and an author that I highly recommend to you. To me, it just doesn't get much better than Dr. Sandra Kennedy. I hope you enjoy her book as much as I did. May God bless you in every way.

—Dr. Jesse Duplantis

INTRODUCTION

Throughout my years in ministry, I have repeatedly encountered people who are hungry for more of God—those who desperately want to quit "playing church" and BE the Church, who long for a closer, deeper relationship with the Lord, to worship and adore their heavenly Father in a new and vibrant way that is truly pleasing to Him. They are willing to do whatever is necessary to achieve this coveted goal.

However, there often seems to be something that blocks them from walking in the fullness of relationship with Him. It is as if something prohibits them from being totally free to worship and serve Him. It prevents them from partaking of all the blessings and benefits God has provided. It hinders them from living a lifestyle that fully expresses the Kingdom of God.

So what is hindering and blocking God's people from rising to higher levels in their walk with God? It is the *stain of sin* that darkens the recesses of one's heart. Despite the fact that they know they have repented before the Lord and their sins are forgiven, there is still this lingering shadow of darkness that prevents them from walking in the fullness of the marvelous light of His love and provisions.

If this describes you, then I have wonderful news—a message that will bring great freedom, peace, and wholeness if you will embrace it. It is the message of *the cleansing, healing power of the Blood of Jesus!*

When we speak about the Blood of Jesus, we are referring to something the Scriptures call *precious*. The precious blood of Jesus has the power to transcend the bonds of sin, sickness, and even death. It is the *only* power that can cleanse us and make us whole, free to walk in and enjoy God's love. The power of the Blood is so miraculous that it will forever be the central theme of our praise and worship of the One who gave His life to redeem us and set us free.

The Blood of Jesus gives us access to a promise of new hope. It's the hope to be cleansed, redeemed, set free, healed, delivered, and protected. It's hope for a new life. It's hope for obtaining all the precious promises of God through faith in Jesus. There is divine power in the Blood each and every time we apply it. Jesus shed His Blood at the Cross of Calvary to neutralize the power of sin, the power of sickness, and the power of death—all the demonic forces of hell. Thank God for the Blood!

No matter whether you are facing condemnation, guilt, the pain of past memories, sickness, or other difficult circumstances, the Blood of Jesus is the key to releasing God's divine power. The Blood of Jesus is the solution to every problem you may encounter. You may have thought of reasons why God would not forgive, save, heal, or deliver you, but you can be sure of one thing—the Blood of Jesus took care of that! It's all about the Blood!

A wonderful excitement fills my heart as I anticipate the moving of God's Spirit in the hearts of those who will receive the truth about the cleansing, healing power of the Blood of Jesus. If you desire a closer relationship with the Father, walking in a higher calling, living in the hope of a better future, cleansed, healed, and free...this message is for you!

CHAPTER 1

WHAT'S WRONG HERE?

I have been teaching God's Word since I was nineteen years old. Over the years, I have seen the Word of God bring change in the lives of many people as well as my own life. Initially, we are often so excited about the Word and its impact, but we all have a tendency to gradually regress into our former habits by letting slip the Word's place of importance in our lives. For whatever reason, we do not stay plugged in to the truths of God. Perhaps we believe that these truths and experiences will carry us the rest of our lives, but they will not unless they are continually embraced and refreshed.

Many years ago, before I accepted God's call into full-time ministry, I spent fourteen years of my life working for my home state of Georgia as a psychologist, therapist, and counselor. During that time, I held the position of district director of mental health and mental retardation centers around the state. While in this capacity, I saw multitudes of people experiencing every imaginable kind of problem. I witnessed the devastation those problems caused in their lives, and how hard it was for them to rebound to normalcy after facing those difficulties.

But the thing that absolutely amazed me, and still does even today, is that as a pastor, I saw the same patterns in the lives of saints that I saw in the world! I still see the same struggles and problems in the Church that I saw outside the Church years ago.

As a whole, I do not see Christians rebounding any faster than those who do not have the Spirit of grace to assist them. To be frank, I often do not see any difference at all, and to me that is a very sad thing. How can this possibly be? We are Christians, in the Body of Christ! We have the Holy Spirit actually living within us. We have been raised up to sit with Him in heavenly places. For us to be in the mess we're in, there must be something terribly wrong.

We must be missing something that God has already provided for us, because Jesus' work on the Cross is complete. There is nothing more that He must accomplish to defeat the devil. We are supposed to be victorious as members of God's elite family.

There are thousands upon thousands of people who claim Jesus as Lord and Savior but are not walking in the power of their salvation. We definitely are not enjoying all the benefits of our salvation, which Jesus shed His Blood to purchase for us. Herein lies the problem: the Word of God and the Blood of Jesus will bring us to a place of total victory. If the

Bible is just a book—an everyday book that we are not really supposed to understand, and are only supposed to read in church on Sunday morning—then let's face it, we are wasting our time.

The Bible is God's Word, and it will accomplish what God sent it to do (Isa. 55:11). We do not need to make things so complicated that only a handful of people are able to comprehend the simplicity of God's Word. We just need to say, "This is what it says; this is what it means; and this is how it works," and *then, with the help of Almighty God, live by it!*

VICTORY

Let me tell you something, I enjoy my salvation. I enjoy being saved! I've been to hell and back a few times, and I can tell you, the trip back is much better. Thank God for the cleansing power of the Blood of the Lamb. He has set me free, glory to God!

I was a mess before Jesus got a hold of me, and I've even been a mess a few times since. But, praise God, the power of the Blood of Jesus has changed my life from deep within. It did not happen overnight. Sometimes it took a little while for the Blood to penetrate, to break through the hardness of unbelief and cleanse me. But eventually it did and brought me victory, thank God. It kept working as long as I kept putting it to work. But in truth, when I stopped, it stopped.

We should be walking on a higher plane than the world. After all, we're supposed to be seated with Jesus in heavenly places (see Eph 2:6). If we are not there, we are the ones who have moved; because according to God's Word, that is where He has seated us.

One of my greatest joys is to look out at the congregation and see people who, like myself, have walked the hard path in life and despite all odds, have made it to a place of victory. I see those who have been in utter darkness, those to whom life has dealt harsh blows. I see those who were in the middle of the sea when the storm hit, and though the storm tried to take them under, they made it to the other side. I love to see God working in the lives of these people. They simply hear what they need to hear, do what they need to do, and God does the rest. God is always faithful.

HOPE

Just by living in this crazy world it is easy to find ourselves in a mess—in a pit with no apparent way out. We normally do not have to go looking very far for trouble. It is highly adept at putting us in its crosshairs. But, hope can begin to flicker deep within us when we embrace the Word of our God; hope not only of escaping the trouble, but hope that God really does not leave us nor forsake us. What a fabulous truth that is! Being a Christian should be synonymous with victory, no matter the source of the trouble.

I have found myself in places when I thought He left me. Have you ever been to that lonesome place where you thought even God had given up on you? Of course, He does not leave us, but it sure feels that way sometimes, doesn't it? We just get so caught up in the situations and circumstances we are facing, that we wind up blocking His actions. Believe me, we have all done it a million times. But, one word from God, one word that pierces our hearts can change our lives in an instant. There should never be hopelessness in God's people; but sadly, I see it all too often. The problem is, we tend to see things as impossible. God never sees impossible.

Today, looking at the headlines of our newspapers, being called a Christian means little; the name is thrown about all too casually. But in my view, if we are going to be called "Christian" after our Lord Jesus, we need to live like Him. It makes no sense for us to go around talking about victory, but not having any real victory in our lives. We have to walk this thing out and be the lights in the dark places of this world. Glory to God, we can do it!

The early Christians certainly lived out their lives with great faith and godliness. Their presence had a tremendous impact on the civilization of their day. The Christlikeness of the new birth was evident and real to them. Their relationship with Jesus was so real to them that everything about them changed. They were overcomers who lived out their faith in such perfection that everybody was either for them or against them—there was no middle ground.

It was very difficult being a Christian back then. We act like it is worse now, but in truth, thousands were killed then just for being faithful to God. They lived persecuted lives, yet the Bible says they turned the world upside down for Christ (see Acts 17:6).

Why is it that in today's world Christians have not been able to make a similar impact and cause the eyes of the world to gaze on this life-changing Jesus within us? Be assured, every victory is always wrapped up in the Blood of the Lamb. In this book, we will press deeper into that immeasurable truth. Praise God!

PRECIOUS AND HOLY

The Blood of Jesus is precious and holy in the sight of Almighty God. After all, it was the sacrifice and death of His beloved Son on the Cross at Calvary that saved us all— every man, woman, and child—from destruction. Once we have learned that, we have the assurance that we can come quickly before the throne, ask forgiveness for our sins, receive that forgiveness, and walk in it.

His Blood is the key to our wonderful salvation and we must embrace it and esteem the Blood with honor. It has the power to bridge the chasm and reconcile unholy people with a Holy God. The Blood of Jesus draws us nigh unto Him and invites us into the household of God as sons and daughters. What a privilege! Glory to His name forever!

The Blood enables God to forgive us of our sins, and to cleanse us from all unrighteousness. That is certainly a true and exciting reality for us. But there is another aspect of the cleansing power of the Blood that I have not heard discussed much.

When the Lord first uncovered this revelation to me, I began remembering crises in my own life through which I had successfully passed. And I discovered with joy that the Lord had been leading me down this pathway a great many years, although I was not consciously aware of it. Isn't it interesting how we can know things in our spirit before we know them in our heads? God's mercy is beyond our comprehension. He is absolutely wonderful.

As I began to teach my church these principles and they began to grasp them and apply them to their own lives, this revelation brought about more change in the hearts of the people than anything I have ever taught. I had never seen so many positive changes take place so fast; it was absolutely astounding. There were so many turnarounds in family situations—turnarounds that actually lasted. Do you know what I mean? We can have turnarounds today, but then tomorrow go back the other way. The changes I have witnessed in the lives of people have kept them going the right way since this teaching on the Blood of Jesus has come forth. It has been amazing.

As a matter of fact, we took a two-week period and did a quick test. We learned how to use the Blood of Jesus as a priest, and apply that precious Blood of the Lamb to situations that were "messed up," and to people who did not know the Lord. Out of the approximately one hundred people who had participated in this test, approximately 70 percent of them saw positive results in that short period of time. Some of these situations and people had been prayed over for years and years; yet in a two-week time period, people saw God change them. Glory!

So, do I have your interest, now? Great! Then let's get started, shall we?

CHAPTER 2

LISTEN UP!

How many of us have had a failure? How many of us have had more than one? It's unanimous, I assure you. Most of us have had more failures than we would like to admit, and all of us have regrets. The Lord showed me one thing in particular, in my own life and in the lives of others, that when we fail or sin and come to Him repentant, we will always receive forgiveness through the shed Blood of Jesus Christ.

Sometimes when we attempt to reestablish our relationship with Him, it seems so difficult to get past our failures. It does not seem to matter how much we pray, how much others pray for us, or how well we understand that God forgives us of our sins and cleanses us from all unrighteousness by the Blood of the Lamb. Most of the time, we just cannot seem to get past our failures. It is like we are always dragging something behind us, or that there is something "dark" hovering over us. Yes, we have certainly asked Jesus to forgive us, and He has been faithful to do just that. But, it seems that "thing" is still there and everybody can see it.

It's like wearing a piece of clothing that we know is stained. It might be that the stain is inconspicuous, but *we* know it's there. It stays with us like a dark cloud and hinders us from walking in the absolute freedom that the Blood of Jesus provides. That, my friend, is the nature of sin. Yet, the Word of God states that the Blood has set us free from sin and the power of that sin.

As I look back through my life, I notice when sins—though forgiven—would get a grip on me and hold me captive. I know that I am not alone. Each of us would have to admit that our past sins continue to haunt us, and we still feel dirty, don't we? We know with our heads that the Blood of Jesus is enough; yet, we think we still ought to somehow pay penance for those transgressions. We feel like we need to do something more, repent again, cry a little more, or tell God how rotten we are—something.

TRULY CLEANSED

I can remember going to camp meetings years ago. I always shied away from meetings with prophets in those days. I never liked going to where the prophets were. I realize there are many who seek out people with that prophetic gift, but I have never been one of them. I was convinced (erroneously, of course) that they would point their finger at me and expose me before the crowd. But the exposure that terrified me concerned sins for which I had already been forgiven. I truly felt that everyone could still see all those things that I had done; it was like I was wearing a "guilty" sign on my forehead. Today, it is a different story; I love prophets! It is wonderful to be clean. I tell you, it is absolutely wonderful to be truly cleansed by the Blood!

So what is the problem? We know that God does not hold our forgiven sin against us. The Bible emphatically declares that. Because of the sacrifice of Jesus, God *chooses* not to remember our sin. Now, *people* continue to hold things against us, but God does not. The work of the Cross has been completed. So what is the problem? Simple. We have not gone deep enough. We are now dealing with the *nature of sin*. We have to look deeper into the power of the Blood of Jesus, and that is the very thing we are going to discuss in this book.

Yes, something *does* attach itself to us. We are going to find out from the Word of God what that something is and how to break its power over us. We are going to find out that we truly are priests before Almighty God, and that we can and should be applying the Blood over ourselves and those who are not walking in victory. Praise God forevermore! But now we need to talk about something else.

DOERS

*Therefore lay aside all filthiness and overflow of wickedness, and receive with meekness the implanted word, which is able to save your souls. But be **doers of the word**, and not hearers only,* *deceiving yourselves. For if anyone is a hearer of the word and not a doer, he is like a man observing his natural face in a mirror; for he observes himself, goes away, and immediately forgets what kind of man he was. But he who looks into the perfect law of liberty and continues in it, and is not a forgetful hearer but a **doer of the work**, this one will be blessed in what he does* (James 1:21-25).

The Bible talks about being doers of the Word and not hearers only. This Scripture in James 1 says that if we want to be blessed, we cannot just hear, we must *do* what we hear! Even if we read and hear the Word every day of the week, if we are not putting those words into practice, we will not reap the benefits of obedience. Many church members are only hearers of God's Word. We sit on the pews, and we hear and hear and hear. By far, the majority of us hear the Word, at least with our natural ears. Churches are saturated with hearers, but hearers do not necessarily "do." People come and hear and some even say, "Yes, amen." Some nod their heads in agreement with what they have heard, while others simply nod their heads and then drift soundly off to sleep. When they leave the sanctuary, they leave everything they have heard on the pew behind them.

As a matter of fact, they think hearing some pastor for one hour a week is far more than enough. Most would say that they are Christians in right-standing with God, but they live the same way they did out in the world.

Is it really possible for God to move into our spirits but no changes take place in our behavior? We cannot walk with God, experience fellowship with God, or understand the things of God and be just a hearer.

God works with those who are hearers *and* doers of the Word. What does that mean? It means applying the Word of God to our day-to-day living. God needs people who not only hear, but do what they hear. To be honest with you, God holds us accountable for a truth once we've heard it and understood it—whether we do it or not. In that situation, our disobedience turns into a curse, meaning God cannot bless us.

We all have a tendency to hear God's Word initially with great excitement; but due to a multitude of reasons, we often quickly let go of the truths we just heard. We must not let go—we must hold on to these great truths. Too often we have an experience with God and gain a degree of freedom, and then we think that will carry us the rest of our life. Not so! Those same besetting sins will begin to come back on us, and we must once again battle for our freedom. The Scripture is very clear, but let me repeat: if we want to be blessed, we must not only be hearers of the Word, but also doers.

Regardless of what is happening in your life right now, if you will actually *do* what the Word says to do, your life will be permanently transformed.

NATURAL INFLUENCES

Let me share with you another one of our problems. Even though we are spirit people, we are so led by what we see, hear, and feel in the natural realm that we are pulled back in that direction. We have to constantly pray and talk to ourselves about being new creatures in Christ Jesus. Let's get really honest, shall we? Surrounded by the power of these natural influences, it is difficult for us to operate with any consistency in the reality of the truth that we really are spirit beings made in the image of Almighty God. All of us struggle with this to some degree or another. Nuggets of God's truth drop into our hearts and we endeavor to hold on to them, but we constantly drop back into the natural realm. Face it—most of us are more tuned in to the natural arena of life because it's more real to us than the world of the spirit.

Victory is a spiritual thing. We tend to believe that victory is tied up in the natural world because we can see the blessings of victory in the lives of people around us, whether it be money, good health, or whatever. But victory does not take place in the natural realm first. It is first birthed in our spirit. Our flesh is an enemy of our spirit; it constantly fights us. Although we will never have complete success ruling our flesh, there is a dimension in which we can truly be overcomers now in this life. It's all wrapped up in what we see and hear. But we need to scrutinize what we see and hear.

Now look with me at Matthew 13:13-15.

Therefore I speak to them in parables, because seeing they do not see, and hearing they do not hear, nor do they understand. And in them the prophecy of Isaiah is fulfilled, which says: "Hearing you will hear and shall not understand, and seeing you will see and not perceive; for the hearts of this people have grown dull. Their ears are hard of hearing, and their eyes they have closed, lest they should see with their eyes and hear with their ears, lest they should understand with their hearts and turn, so that I should heal them."

Now, we understand that God created us to walk in truth—to walk in His image—but people dulled their ears and closed their eyes. Write this on the tablet of your heart: we were made to walk with God and hear Him speaking to us. Think about how wonderful that is. He desires to share His heart with us and communicate with us as friends! *Oh my—Lord Jesus, You are so good to us. Thank You.*

It remains true that we can turn off our ears and choose not to hear and reject the truth, as the Scripture passage in Matthew 13 so clearly states. When we do that, we leave ourselves vulnerable for our hearts to be hardened and to be tempted to fall away from God. When we reject God's truth, we become spiritually blind and deaf. It does not matter how saved we are. We will start stumbling, walking about in darkness. This is not about going to Heaven after we die, it is about Christians rejecting the truth they have heard, and refusing to allow it to change their lives.

There is a multitude of reasons why we do that. Sometimes, the truth does not line up with what we have been taught. Or it may not agree with denominational doctrines that we are aligned with, or we may know somebody for whom the Word did not "seem to work." No matter the reason, excuses will only keep us from walking in victory in a way that exemplifies the abundant life that Jesus died to give us.

When we hear a message and say, "Wow, that was good!" yet we fail to apply the principles to our daily lives, we need to beware, for we are inviting spiritual blindness and deafness. In one sense, every time we refuse to be doers of the Word, we are saying that we do not consider the Word important enough to be put into practice in our lives. Perhaps it would be to our advantage to reread the history of Israel and the examples of the Old Covenant that were written for our instruction.

LEARNING AND DISCERNING

In the same way we can reject truth, we can also embrace lies. We must learn to compare what we hear and see—and even what we already believe—against what God's Word actually says. We can be sincere, yet be sincerely wrong and believe something completely contrary to the Word. While we love and honor our pastors, we need to read and find out what the Word of God says for ourselves. I'll let you in on a secret. This may shock you, but *we pastors don't know everything!* Surprised? I know it is hard to believe, but yes, it's true! We are just people, like you, but people to whom God has given the huge responsibility of shepherding His flock. Be assured, we always need to be learning for ourselves what the Word says. Now, let's look at another important Scripture.

Beware, brethren, lest there be in any of you an evil heart of unbelief, in departing from the living God (Hebrews 3:12).

This passage is not written to the sinner, but to those in the Church who have made Jesus Christ the Lord of their lives. That's us. And it says that we better take heed. An evil heart of unbelief can cause us to depart from the living God. That is a pretty serious warning! When we begin to think that a situation or a circumstance occurring in our life is bigger than the power of God, we have, at that moment, allowed a seed of unbelief to be planted within us

We may experience a jolt of unbelief when some horrendous thing hits us, and we can be thrown off balance at first. But however long we stay tuned in to that unbelief depends on what is actually in our heart at the time. If we stay tuned to the negative side of life, we are watering seeds of unbelief that will produce negative thoughts and emotions within us. I am telling you, this is very frightening because we live in a world that is saturated with negativism. Naturally speaking, all of us tend to go that way, but negativism works against God in our lives. We really have to exert the effort and strive to stay centered on faith.

I assure you, that if we really knew what dangers we were dealing with through unbelief, we would refuse to allow it to operate in our lives! Our God is a God of possibilities, and the Blood of Jesus can turn a negative heart into a positive power for God and His Kingdom. Glory to God forevermore!

Now consider this before we move on. Unbelief is a sin. It's the major sin that can keep people out of Heaven. It's the one that grieves the heart of God relating to His own children. Have your children ever attacked your integrity when you've always acted uprightly with them? It is very hurtful when they refuse to hear your heart. God is the perfect Father. He has never hurt us, let us down, or failed to be there for us, yet we act and talk like He has. He simply wants us to trust Him and believe the Word He has spoken to us. Not all that unreasonable, is it? We need to believe and live in the realm of what God can do and leave unbelief behind.

FREEDOM

We must understand and thoroughly grasp the truth that God wants us free. I am often amazed by the fact that to many people that idea is so foreign. I've thought about this many times—it must be terribly hard trying to serve God when you believe that He is the One who has caused all of your trouble. What is so disturbing to me is the number of *His own people* who believe that He is at the root of their problems. God is not our trouble. Let me say it again! God is not our trouble. He never has been and never will be! God really does want us to be free. That is why He sent Jesus to us. Think about it. We were already in eternal bondage through sin; already destined for destruction. God did not need to send Jesus to be our Deliverer if He wanted us to remain in bondage.

Our chains of bondage are not the result of the hand of God. If we are experiencing any type of bondage keeping us from victory, it is not God's doing or His will for our lives. It is the result of ignorance and unbelief concerning what the Blood of Jesus can do in our lives. It is absolutely crucial that we look at the Word and understand the power of the Blood of Jesus.

Some of us think we have things so terribly wrong with us that the Blood cannot reach us, much less change what is wrong in our lives. We've believed lies satan has told us about ourselves. We have bought into those lies and accepted them as truth, then we have pulled away from God in shame.

Satan is a liar and a loser—don't ever accept the lies he throws your way! I know that may be easier said than done, but we are going to get into the Bible and accept what *it* says. I will say it again—there are no impossible situations with God! He yearns to lift us up and give us victory over every obstacle in life. Praise God!

Oh, I know bad things come our way. Every one of us has difficulties and faces potentially despairing circumstances, and those circumstances try to grab us and wrestle us down. But they cannot do it—they do not have the power to do it *unless we let them* take hold of us and gain control. Too often we allow a situation to rule our lives. It is time for us to take a stand of authority in the name of Jesus. It is high time we rule the situation by His authority and see the power of God excel on our behalf.

SLIP SLIDING AWAY

We must take heed of that warning; we cannot afford to have hearts filled with unbelief, or even the prospect of falling away from God. I am sure you, like me, have tried to change your heart; and if we could have changed the hearts of others, we would have done it years ago, right?

For whatever reason, it is very liberating for me to know I cannot change my heart. I've been in battles—big battles—heart-versus-flesh battles. I truly loved God, but I still struggled. I wanted to serve God, but found myself pulling away from God. I did not want to pray or read God's wonderful Word, and sometimes I even wanted to call the church and tell them I would not be there. Then it dawned on me, I was the preacher! I *had* to be there!

I do not remember a time after my new birth when I just sat up at night and planned a way to walk away from Him. I do not ever remember writing out some kind of way to get back into sin. I just slowly, but surely, slipped away from the things of God, just got side-tracked. Unfortunately, once we get on that slippery slope leading us away from God, it is easy to just keep sliding.

Satan is a liar and a deceiver. He never tricks us head-on—he always attacks from the rear. If we are not ever watchful to walk with God, or if we are not tuned in to the Spirit of

God, we can very easily be deceived. And once deceived, our hearts will begin to turn from God.

Just to be clear, having an impure or evil heart does not make us evil people. Every time we are outside of faith, we are in unbelief and could therefore be considered to have an "evil" or unregenerate heart.

The medical field is an area of concern here. We thank God for the medical profession and the wisdom that they have to help us. But many times they call us "terminal" when God's Word emphatically states that we are the healed. When we believe a doctor's word more than we believe what God has said in His Word, we are out of line. Our minds have a tendency to say to us, "I am not evil; I love God." I am not talking about an evil act here, but about a heart, meaning our mind and thoughts, which is contrary to the Word and will of God. We get into an arena of unbelief where we are not trusting God.

Any distraction that comes our way, trying to get us to follow after something other than God's Word, has the potential to lead us away from God and into trouble if we are not careful. God's Word must be our final authority—no matter what else we may hear. We only see symptoms and circumstances, but God knows the root of our problem and how to deal with it.

When we get distracted and off course from the pathways of wisdom found in God's Word, one thing leads to another and we find ourselves disoriented, confused, and discouraged because we lose hope. We need God to empower us to live victoriously in this crazy world! Quite often though, even after we repent, we still have trouble getting back to our former spiritual level.

Let's find out why.

CHAPTER 3

FEELING DIRTY?

*When He had called all the multitude to Himself, He said to them, "Hear Me, everyone, and understand: There is nothing that enters a man from outside which can **defile** him; but the things which come out of him, those are the things that **defile** a man. If anyone has ears to hear, let him hear!" When He had entered a house away from the crowd, His disciples asked Him concerning the parable. So He said to them, "Are you thus without understanding also? Do you not perceive that whatever enters a man from outside cannot **defile** him, because it does not enter his heart but his stomach, and is eliminated, thus purifying all foods?" And He said, "What comes out of a man, that **defiles** a man. For from within, out of the heart of men, proceed evil thoughts, adulteries, fornications, murders, thefts, covetousness, wickedness, deceit, lewdness, an evil eye, blasphemy, pride, foolishness. All these evil things come from within and **defile** a man"* (Mark 7:14-23).

As I studied these verses in Mark 7, my question was, "What is meant by the word *defile?*" I found out that there are approximately sixteen Greek and Hebrew words that are translated "defile." We are going to focus on the four most common ones through various Scripture passages and examine what each has to do with the cleansing power of the Blood of Jesus.

One of those four words is found in this passage of Scripture in Mark 7. The Greek translation for the word *defile* in these verses means "to make common." Sinful behavior, such as covetousness, deceit, and pride, are things that defile us and make us common. But the truth of the matter is—we are not common. We are to walk uprightly, unlike mere mortals—because we are made in the image of God. When we participate in those behaviors of the world, we *become* common. And when we become common, we are no longer godly. It is impossible to be godly and common at the same time. If we have participated in those activities to any degree, we can be totally forgiven and not yet totally cleansed.

But hang on now. I am not coming against the Blood of Jesus in any way. In the eyes of God, we are completely forgiven at the spirit level, but the residue of that sin hangs on in our hearts, meaning our soulish area. I thought the heart and the spirit were one and the same for the longest time. But after long study, I discovered that is not necessarily true in every incident. We will get into that later.

When we walk in pride or walk in foolishness, we are walking like a common, unregenerate person. Let me put it another way. We are walking like a common, defiled person when we, for example, participate in evil thoughts. If we keep our minds on evil thoughts, those thoughts will eventually get down into our hearts. We're not talking about the crazy thoughts that sweep through our minds—those wild things that hit our conscious thinking and make us ask ourselves, *Where did that come from?* I am talking about those evil thoughts that we dwell on, focus on, and do not cast down as the Bible says we are supposed to.

How do we experience these evil thoughts? Well, they can occur when we start thinking about somebody else's husband or wife in an ungodly manner, or dwell on thoughts of doing harm to another. Those are pretty obvious, aren't they? Let's get down to more subtle ways. Do we rejoice when harm comes to someone who has hurt us, thinking it serves the person right? Come on now, be honest. When we behave like that, we are common—no different from the world. We are not to rejoice when anything harmful or evil comes against any person. Read First Corinthians 13 to know how God wants us to think, feel, and act about others.

We know that fornication, murder, and theft are wrong. Ah, but what about thoughts like, *Why doesn't the pastor ever let me sing? Why doesn't he let me teach? Why doesn't the pastor realize I have the ability? I could do a better job than so and so.* My friend, that is the beginning of covetousness that started with an evil thought. And what about all of those evil, hateful, or haughty looks? Some people have such an evil eye that they may not say a word, but their look is enough to kill. *Lord Jesus, help us.*

I love to watch people during our prayer times because it is a good time to see how people react. Everybody is on different spiritual levels. I know that. I don't get upset if somebody prays something that might not be quite on target. I'm just glad they are praying. I agree with what is right, and I disagree with what is wrong, but I don't faint and fall on the floor when someone prays in error. We need to remember, we all have prayed like that in times past. Let's get honest, shall we? Once we are born again, we have to learn how to pray accurately, and that takes time.

It bothers me when people get to a self-appointed place where they judge others with their little motions and little doings like rolling their eyes in disgust or ridicule because others are not on their spiritual level. God never appointed any of us to sit on the judge's bench. We are not to be or act common, but to undergird and help each other grow up in the things of the Lord.

We did not just wake up one morning as spiritual giants. None of us is there, I assure you. But we are on our way, hallelujah! Sin defiles us because we are not reflecting the image of God that is within us.

SIN DEFILES

Now, let's look at another Scripture about defilement.

*Behold, the Lord's hand is not shortened, that it cannot save; nor His ear heavy, that it cannot hear. But your iniquities have separated you from your God; and your sins have hidden His face from you, so that He will not hear. For your hands are **defiled** with blood, and your fingers with iniquity; your lips have spoken lies, your tongue has muttered perversity* (Isaiah 59:1-3).

The word translated *defiled* here means "stained." So, defilement of any kind makes us stained. Sin always leaves a stain. Now listen—*repentance* does not mean "remove the stain," because repentance is simply changing direction. Repentance is when we stop heading in one direction, make an about-face, and head in the opposite direction. That is repentance. But we can be going one way in sin, stop, and begin going another way, and yet the stain of that sin remains within us. That's what's been wrong with a lot of us Christians.

We've repented and repented and repented for the same thing, and we were forgiven by our gracious heavenly Father the very first time we confessed it. Yet, the stain of that sin has made us feel like we were clothed in shame.

Oh yes, there is a way to remove that stain, but repentance does not *automatically* remove the stain. This should help us understand what has happened to us in days past and why we feel the way we do. And with the help of the Lord Jesus Christ, we are going to learn how to walk forever free of those stains. Glory to God! He is so merciful to us. His divine provision is beyond our wildest dreams, and His love is stronger than our deepest sin.

Let's take a look at the book of Genesis.

*And when Shechem the son of Hamor the Hivite, prince of the country, saw her, he took her, and lay with her, and **defiled** her* (Genesis 34:2 KJV).

The word translated *defiled* here means "to force to submit to uncleanness or to make one dirty." Let's recap: defilement makes us common, causes stains, and makes us dirty. We can absolutely be covered with "spiritual" dirt; that's why we need the Blood of Jesus cleansing us continually.

*Behold, therefore, I will bring strangers against you, the most terrible of the nations; and they shall draw their swords against the beauty of your wisdom, and **defile** your splendor* (Ezekiel 28:7).

In this instance, the word *defile* means "to wound, such as to lay open, give access to, to cut something open." When we become defiled by sin, there is a wound that appears—not just a bruise, but an open wound within us.

Let's recall that natural things teach us spiritual truths. Jesus often used the natural realm to explain heavenly principles. If our body has an open wound and it gets dirty, what happens to it? It gets infected, doesn't it? *("Whoever has ears, let them hear what the Spirit says..." Revelation 2:17.)* Infection sets in. Now, when we repent and change direction, we still can have an open wound or a spiritual infection from deep within us that needs attention. If we do not stay under the teaching of sound doctrine, are not undergirded and supported by our brothers and sisters in the Lord, or do not allow time for healing and cleansing to take place, we regress, we fall back into our former behaviors. We are critically vulnerable if we do not allow God to take care of the wound—and cleanse it with the Blood of the Lamb.

SIN STAINS

Sin is treacherous and the stain of sin is just as serious. Too many of God's people have thought they can live however they want and not only make it to Heaven, but walk in God's fullness day to day just because they once made a confession of faith to a pastor long ago. It is impossible to walk upright, manifesting the glory of the Lord while remaining defiled. We may have wondrous mountain-top experiences; we may fly like eagles—but then crash land like a turkey.

It has happened to all of us at one time or another. Thank God He has made provision for us to be overcomers and walk in victory daily. Glory to God! He's laid a path for it and given us the instruction and the power to do it. I'm telling you that we are going to walk in victory, and we are going to do it right. The glorious Church will rise above this thing to the glory of God the Father, and show this dying world the goodness of Jehovah, the King of the universe.

This is Good News, to discover the provision God has made for us to walk free. I know because I have felt wounded. I have felt stained. I have felt dirty. And I have certainly felt common. This is shouting ground! Oh, I am so glad that the residue, the stain of any and all sin, can be washed away by the Blood of Jesus. Hallelujah!

A very noted and anointed evangelist credited with preaching that has literally brought millions of people into the Kingdom of God has said that in the follow-up efforts, his ministry is not able to find the majority of the people who went forward to get saved during his meetings. They repented all right, but there was still something that greatly hindered them from attending church or moving forward with God.

All of us need to be admonished to give God our whole life, attend a good church that preaches the full Gospel, and be consistent there so we can be healed of all the mess within us. If we dedicate ourselves to God in such a manner, we can walk in victory. But if we bounce in and out and come and go at our convenience, we will get sidetracked. If we do not stay centered on God's Word and His principles, we are going to get lost in the shuffle and remain wounded.

We'll find ourselves resentful of others, especially those who have remained faithful and are now way ahead of us spiritually. Watch out if you start saying, "I don't want to go to church. I don't believe I have to be at church all the time...blah, blah, blah." When you hear yourself saying such things, you can know you are moving backward, not forward with God.

People who say those kinds of things will not walk in victory. Because they do not know what else to do, they will lash out at you. When they see changes in your life—how you are excelling and how things seem to be going well for you—and because they are not willing to do those same things, they will begin to say hurtful, negative things.

There are certain spiritual aspects of our lives that must be tended to daily, and most of them must be tended over a period of time to be fully restored. We have to *stick with the program* to walk in victory. It takes time to work things out that are deep within us. If everyone who has ever gone to the altar in our church and repented were still attending our services, we would have to meet at the downtown stadium. Like most churches, we are unable to keep up with them; they just come and go, come and go. Believers have to dedicate themselves to a new lifestyle; and Jesus will be there to see that we are victorious! Glory to God!

This is a one-sided fight, but not enough of us seem to know it. God is always on our side. It gives Him great pleasure when He sees us put the devil under our feet. It is God's great pleasure to give us the Kingdom. Hallelujah!

> *Alas, sinful nation, a people laden with iniquity, a brood of evildoers, children who are corrupters! They have forsaken the Lord, they have provoked to anger the Holy One of Israel, they have turned away backward. Why should you be stricken again? You will revolt more and more. The whole head is sick, and the whole heart faints. From the sole of the foot even to the head, there is no soundness in it, but wounds and bruises and putrefying sores; they*

*have not been closed or bound up, or soothed with
ointment* (Isaiah 1:4-6).

This Scripture passage in Isaiah 1 is a picture of what the
Church looks like when laden with sin. Keep in mind the
fact that this passage is talking about God's people, the ones
who are supposed to know better. Oh yes, there are defilements present within the Church, and we have not given
them time for their healing to occur.

A GOOD WASHING

*To what purpose is the multitude of your sacrifices
to Me?" says the Lord. "I have had enough of burnt
offerings of rams and the fat of fed cattle. I do not
delight in the blood of bulls, or of lambs or goats....
Wash yourselves, make yourselves clean; put away
the evil of your doings from before My eyes. Cease to
do evil"* (Isaiah 1:11,16).

The key to turning all of these situations around is the
washing. Whether we're dirty, wounded, common, or stained,
we need a good washing—not just a good cover-up, but a
thorough washing. We need something that is going to take
that mess, that defilement, away from us. Let me tell you,
washing is not a one-time experience—neither in the natural or the spiritual realms. Regrettably, there have been some
who have tried that, and we can always smell them coming!
Washing must be done on a continuous basis in both the
natural and the spiritual.

There are some good Scriptures in the Bible about washing. Let me share just a few of them with you.

Have mercy upon me, O God, according to Your lovingkindness; according to the multitude of Your tender mercies, blot out my transgressions. **Wash me thoroughly** *from my iniquity, and cleanse me from my sin* (Psalm 51:1-2).

Behold, I will bring it health and healing; I will heal them and reveal to them the abundance of peace and truth. And I will cause the captives of Judah and the captives of Israel to return, and will rebuild those places as at the first. I will **cleanse** *them from all their iniquity by which they have sinned against Me, and I will pardon all their iniquities by which they have sinned and by which they have transgressed against Me. Then it shall be to Me a name of joy, a praise, and an honor before all nations of the earth, who shall hear all the good that I do to them; they shall fear and tremble for all the goodness and all the prosperity that I provide for it* (Jeremiah 33:6-9).

Husbands, love your wives, just as Christ also loved the church and gave Himself for her, that He might sanctify and **cleanse** *her with the* **washing** *of water by the word, that He might present her to Himself a glorious church, not having spot or wrinkle or any* *such thing, but that she should be holy and without blemish* (Ephesians 5:25-27).

*John, to the seven churches which are in Asia: Grace to you and peace from Him who is and who was and who is to come, and from the seven Spirits who are before His throne, and from Jesus Christ, the faithful witness, the firstborn from the dead, and the ruler over the kings of the earth. To Him who loved us and **washed** us from our sins in His own blood, and has made us kings and priests to His God and Father, to Him be glory and dominion forever and ever. Amen* (Revelation 1:4-6).

Now, let's look at First John 1:7-8:

*But if we walk in the light as He is in the light, we have fellowship with one another, and the blood of Jesus Christ His Son **cleanses** us from all sin. If we say that we have no sin, we deceive ourselves, and the truth is not in us.*

Look at the word *cleanses* in verse 7. Interestingly, it denotes a continuous cleansing as we walk in the light of His Word and by the Blood of Jesus. I believe that is the loophole with which satan has deceived the Church. We are to be cleansed daily by the Blood of the Lamb, yet we have thought this cleansing needed to occur only at the moment of our new birth and that was it.

I was raised Baptist. I cherish my Baptist background and my ordination papers are still with the Baptist church. As I grew up and experienced life and failure, I got "saved" many times. I know we can only get saved once, but I felt unclean and stained by my shortcomings even after repenting. I simply did not know what else to do.

Can you identify with this struggle to be free? I repeatedly asked the Lord to come back into my heart, hoping to experience the same freedom as when I first got saved. The truth is, I did not need to get saved again because Jesus never actually left me; neither will He leave you. How many of us have crawled to altars, sobbing our hearts out, begging for forgiveness, and trying to get saved again to be restored to God.

The truth is, we get tainted in life by what occurs around us. We continue to miss the mark of excellence set by God's standards. Knowing that God does not flow through dirty vessels, is it any wonder that when we go and lay hands on the sick nothing happens?

I'm going to share with you something I believe you'll shout about! You will learn how to wash yourself in the Blood of the Lamb as a priest and walk free and clean of every defilement. Praise God forevermore!

Stay with me…it gets even better!

CHAPTER 4

FULFILLING THE LAW

Do not think that I came to destroy the Law or the Prophets. I did not come to destroy but to fulfill (Matthew 5:17).

Jesus is the fulfillment of the law; that is certainly the truth. As born-again children of God, we know that, don't we? In this age of grace, we like to shout, "I am not under the law," but the law is really not a bad thing. The law describes a lifestyle that is pleasing to God, but seemingly tough to keep. The problem I see in the Church is that we have been ignorant of what Jesus fulfilled for us. We need to know what He fulfilled so we can walk in every blessing, or His work is useless to us.

Hosea 4:6 says that God's people are destroyed for a lack of knowledge. We are not required to live under the letter of the law because Jesus fulfilled the law. We will not be held under its bondage of rules and regulations. We are grateful we do not have that obligation because Old Covenant saints had difficulty fully keeping it.

However, the spirit of the law is different. It is hugely advantageous for us to have a working knowledge of its principles, just as we would from any Old Covenant passages, such as those in Isaiah, Proverbs, and the Psalms.

As New Testament saints, we live and move and have our being mainly in the Epistles, but that does not negate the truths dispersed throughout the rest of the Bible. The New Testament simply completes and explains the old. And although Jesus fulfilled the law two thousand years ago, we are certainly involved in its fulfillment today through Him. Can we grasp what a privilege that is to be involved in the work of God on earth? When we know what belongs to us, we can shout from the housetops, "Thank God. Jesus fulfilled the law for me. Glory to His name!"

Thank You, dear Jesus. Because of Your mighty work, I take great pride in walking in the fulfillment of the law. Hallelujah!

To look the devil square in the face with boldness, and tell him in no uncertain terms that we are free of sin and that we will not take the burden or shame of it again, requires knowledge of the law and what Jesus has fulfilled. It makes a notable difference how we respond to life's situations when we have a clear understanding of the provisions of Calvary.

Although God writes His Commandments on the tablets of our hearts, we still need to be familiar with the law.

For instance, we need to know that the Jewish holy days were set down by the law. These days are called the Feasts of the Lord. Question: Whose feasts are they? God instructed the Jewish people to celebrate these festivals, but obviously they were God's feasts because they were known as the Feasts of the Lord: *"Speak to the children of Israel, and say to them: 'The feasts of the Lord, which you shall proclaim to be holy convocations, these are My feasts'"* (Lev. 23:2). It becomes extremely interesting when we look up two particular Hebrew words in this verse. One of the main meanings of the word *feast* is "appointment." The other word is *convocations*, which means an "assembly," but it also means a "rehearsal." Could it be that these feast days are God's appointed times to do something specific while He commands the Jews to celebrate or rehearse them yearly? That revelation by itself is an eye opener, knowing that God has appointments that He will accomplish on a certain day at a certain time!

I tell you again, Jesus fulfilled the law, and He fulfilled the required spring festivals of Passover, the Feast of Unleavened Bread, the Feast of First Fruits, and Pentecost—to the day and hour as set down in the law! Glory to God!

The spring festivals set the precedence, and undoubtedly in time, the fall festivals will be fulfilled in the same preciseness. The next one to be fulfilled is the Feast of Trumpets. We know what happens when the trumpet is blown, don't we? The rapture! Glory to God and hallelujah!

The Feast of Tabernacles is another that has yet to be fulfilled in God's appointment book, when God literally comes down and tabernacles, resides, with His people! But it is coming, according to the law. We know it will happen during the millennial Kingdom, but the Jews celebrate it every year according to the law.

Gentiles have observed some of the holy days and not others. Just the same, God gave us *all* of them in the law. We are not under the law or required to obey all of the rituals of the feasts, but if these holy days give us a "calendar" for coming events, wouldn't it behoove us to at least be familiar with them? God's Word is full of nuggets of wisdom of His plan for the coming days. Praise God forever!

CONTINUAL CLEANSING

There is a part of the law that we are concentrating on in this book. Let's take a look at it:

> *Now this is what you shall offer on the altar: two lambs of the first year, day by day* **continually***. One lamb you shall offer in the morning, and the other lamb you shall offer at twilight* (Exodus 29:38-39).

Here is one sacrifice that God said does not stop. As a matter of fact, if we read Jewish history, we discover that there was an attempt to stop this particular sacrifice during Daniel's time, and was successfully halted at the end of the Roman season. Hebrew historians state that when Babylon forced Israel to stop these morning and evening sacrifices, the greatest devastations, the greatest impacts, occurred.

Check out the word *continually*. It actually means "perpetually, it shall never cease." Under the Old Covenant, this event was called the morning and evening sacrifice, and it happened each and every day. Priests had to ceremonially wash in the blood morning and evening. Jesus fulfilled this part of the law too, and is *still fulfilling* it even today for us in the spirit dimension!

For us, the Lamb was slain at Calvary's Cross; there is no further need for sacrifices. But today, He is still our Morning and Evening Sacrifice in the Spirit realm. How do we partake of this sacrifice? By applying His Blood to our lives each day with the words of our confession—morning and evening—because the Old Testament sacrifice was that of blood. If the blood of sacrificial animals was able to accomplish what it did as a type and symbol of the Lamb that was to come, how much more is the living Blood of Jesus able to accomplish this cleansing for us today?

If we are not daily applying the Blood, we are walking around defiled, common, stained, and wounded. Today, we walk out in the Spirit what they did in the natural under the Old Covenant. When we walk around defiled, we experience a "power shortage" in our lives because God needs to work through clean vessels. Truly, we have not understood the power in the Blood of Jesus that belongs to us and what it can accomplish. It was required for priests to wash daily. We are going to find out that we are priests unto God in

Christ Jesus, our Lord, and that we can and should be operating in that office as born-again children of God. We will
be absolutely amazed at our responsibilities and privileges.

> *If we say that we have fellowship with Him, and
> walk in darkness, we lie and do not practice the
> truth. But if we walk in the light as He is in the
> light, we have fellowship with one another, and the
> **blood** of Jesus Christ His Son **cleanses** us from all
> sin* (1 John 1:6-7).

The word *cleanses* in this passage from First John 1 is not
a one-time happening, but an ongoing process. There is to
be a continuous cleansing by the Blood of the Lamb in our
lives. Just as we wash ourselves daily in the natural, we are to
be cleansed from contaminants by the Blood of the Lamb in
the spirit dimension. Jesus fulfilled the law. He did not wipe
it out. Today, we partake of it freely, not under the letter of
the law, but under the Spirit of the law. Thank You, Jesus!

WASH IN THE BLOOD

Most of us are carrying around a lot of baggage that holds
us back from being the glorious Church He foreordained
us to be. We are stained, common, dirty, and wounded. It
could have been a wound that took place twenty years ago,
but we're still carrying it around with us. We have probably
learned how to cover it up and hide it from others, but it continues to unmercifully hang around our neck and come up at
us in the night hours. We find ourselves, in our quiet time,

endeavoring to praise God in spirit and truth—when there it is again, slapping us in the face. Even the emotions resurrect, and again we cower before our God in disgrace and shame.

What do we do? We repent again as tears stream down our face over a sin long ago forgiven and cleansed by the Blood of the Lamb. Then we repent long enough to start feeling all right again. Many of us have been there. It is a familiar scene because we have not understood what Jesus has done for us. We are to wash ourselves in the Blood of the Lamb, morning and evening. We are to wash ourselves and give Him praise because the mighty Blood of the Lamb conquers the stain and heals the wound. Praise His Holy name forever! He is so wonderful!

There is nothing in our lives that the Blood of Jesus Christ has not already conquered. It does not matter what our problem is or what situation we may be facing. The answer is emphatically the Blood of Jesus. It is the strongest power in the world. While working hand in glove with the exchanges at Calvary and the name of the Lord Jesus, this Trio will get the job done—and done right.

UNSPOTTED FROM THE WORLD

In the same light, there are those who would say, "I haven't committed any sin. I don't need cleansing." I hope sin is not part of our lifestyle before God and others, but we are not as holy as we think we are. Look at the world in which we live. We live in a cesspool. This world is full of corruption and defilements. Daily we are bombarded by its degradations. In the same way, we do not necessarily have to wallow in the mud to take a bath in the natural. Our day could have been spent in an office building where there was no mud puddle, but we take a bath because we feel dirty just from the environment, the fallen world. Look at this:

> *Pure and undefiled religion before God and the Father is this: to visit orphans and widows in their trouble, and to keep oneself unspotted from the world* (James 1:27).

Notice this verse did not say to keep ourselves unspotted from sin. It directs us to keep ourselves *"unspotted from the world."* Look at it again. I was amazed when I saw that. I looked up the word *world,* and discovered that it means "the influence from the world's systems and its ungodly multitudes." We are to keep ourselves from the evil influences of the world, because being in this world contaminates and deposits filth upon us. We are to keep ourselves cleansed and unspotted from the influences of the world and its ungodliness. What is ungodly around us, corrupts us.

Here is another verse saying the same thing. This is part of Jesus' prayer in the Garden of Gethsemane to the Father before His crucifixion, and the Bible uses the very same word:

> *I pray not that thou shouldest take them out of the world, but that thou shouldest keep them from the evil* (John 17:15 KJV).

The word *evil* here means two things in the New Testament. One is the act that we do. The other is the influence of an ungodly corrupting world (not an act of sin). Jesus prayed that God would keep us from the ungodly influence of the world, not just take us out of it. We need to be the lights in the midst of this dark world.

The world we live in, my friend, is a mess—a cesspool of evil contaminants that will attach themselves to us should we allow it. We need to wash and cleanse ourselves of these things. We can do it. Jesus has already helped us. He prayed that God would help us to stay clean from the evil influences of the world in which we live. Surely His prayers were heard and answered, don't you think?

There are only two things identified in the Bible that will wash and cleanse us—the Word and the Blood. Most believers have learned over the years how to get into the Word and be washed with the living water of the Word. But I don't think we know how to be washed and cleansed by the Blood. We do that by applying the Blood. I don't think the Church as a whole has the understanding of the importance of the morning and evening cleansing by the precious Blood of the Lord Jesus. Oh, we sing about the Blood all right, but I am talking about making the power of the Blood work in our lives. The power in our lives comes from our ability to apply the Word of God combined with the relationship we have with Jesus Christ. Yet, the application of the Blood is the source of our cleansing to do such things.

REALLY CLEAN?

We are born again, but are we clean? The power we exhibit in our lives depends on our relationship with Jesus and how clean we are. The evil influence of the world will taint us and make us unclean for the ministry that God has called us to accomplish. Among other things, our ears, mouth, hands, and eyes must be cleansed by the Blood daily. We must learn to be clean vessels for the days ahead. We cannot just flip-flop from dirty to clean when the notion strikes us.

Many come to church cursing at their spouse in the car, then walk into church and say, "Hallelujah!" and think everything is all right with God simply because they changed faces walking in the door. Then they leave after the service and talk about how much God was in that service. That, my friend, is a sad joke. All they have experienced is some fleshly moment, not an experience with God, because God is holy and His true presence brings conviction of ungodly behavior.

God pointed out that very thing to me about my own life. He identified all of the wasted preaching and teaching I did over the years under the pretense that God was in it. He revealed the many times when I stood before His people to preach and I had not been walking uprightly before Him. I believed there was a move of God and that something was happening among the people. His Word did not return unto Him void, but most assuredly, the meeting was not as it should have been.

Whatever our calling, whether in the fivefold ministry or whether we play an instrument, or usher at the door, or whatever, we must live right by the power of the Holy Spirit. Most of us believe like I did, and think that we can just say, "God, forgive me," but with no change of behavior, we will be clean and holy. Wrong! We have to learn to live not only tighter with God, but learn how to apply the Blood of Jesus as a bath.

We cannot live like the devil—cussing and carrying on, tearing people down with gossip—and then plead, "Forgive me, Jesus" and think that little "so called" repentance is a stamp of approval from God. Certainly many have done just that in one way or another. We must bow before Him, repent (earnestly change directions) with all of our hearts, and receive our cleansing. I am talking about our *Holy* God, not Joe Blow down the street. I am talking about Jehovah, the Creator of heaven and earth. We are talking about the God of eternity who has cherubim and angels around Him who say nothing but "Holy, holy, holy."

Yet we come be-bopping into the church service after living a sloppy, carnal life all week, lift our hands toward Heaven and think we have entered into the presence of God. We have not. I tell you, it would be grim for us if it were not for the provisions of God and the Blood of Jesus. Thank God for His mercy toward us!

When this truth came as revelation to me, I publicly asked God to forgive me, and asked the people to forgive me for the times I preached or laid hands on them and did not fully understand the seriousness of my actions. I was ignorant, just absolutely ignorant. He has been so gracious to me.

LIFE AND DEATH

We are talking about life and death issues here. We are talking about the God who is calling us to Himself, so that our hands can be an expression of Him and His everlasting love to others. The Bible does not say that the New Testament saints extended their hands. It says they extended *His* hands. The glorious Church is to be like Him. We were created to think like Him, to walk like Him, and talk like Him through the provision of the life-changing Blood of the Lamb. If we will learn to bathe in it, we can experience a cleansing beyond our wildest dreams.

The Blood will break the power of that thing we have been dragging around. Certainly, repentance is the first step, but then we need to go further and bathe ourselves in the Blood and watch what will happen! Oh, how we need to appreciate and honor His precious Blood! The Blood flows from Immanuel's veins to remove the stains, the wounds, the dirt, and the commonness and make us whole to the glory of God the Father. Thank You, Jesus. You are so wonderful. We are to keep Jesus vibrant in our hearts and allow Him to take an active role and lead us step-by-step.

Here is one danger we face. Although we are born again and have the Spirit of grace abiding in our hearts, we allow our hearts to leave Him first, and then our feet follow. The prodigal son left in his heart (soulish area: the mind, will, and emotions) before he ever took a physical step away from his home and father. The application of the Blood is instrumental in maintaining an intimate relationship with God.

We have learned how to plead the Blood of Jesus over ourselves for protection. We have done it for years. God is revealing to us now that there is another dimension available to us that satan has blinded us from. We have pled the Blood for safety, but the Blood has to be applied for cleansing in the Spirit realm. My Bible teaches me that if my hands are not clean, God does not even hear me when I pray. I have to be clean, and He did not mean physical hands. We are talking about a heart issue.

Now let's talk about the heart and spirit.

CHAPTER 5

WHAT IS THE HEART ANYWAY?

W e have taught for years that the heart and the spirit
are the same, yet we must remember to keep it in
context. There are a couple of instances in the Scripture
when the words are used interchangeably. In fact, without
doing a little bit of studying on the words *heart* and *spirit*,
we would not know they were different in the first place.
But I guarantee you, most of the time we see *heart* in the
Old Testament Scriptures, it does not mean a person's
"spirit."

First of all, if we are born again, our *spirit* is the part
of us that underwent the great transformation the moment
we were born into God's family. Our spirit is then turned
toward Christ and to the things of God. He resides in our
born-again spirit. Remember, this is a New Testament fulfillment for those who are born again. If the heart and spirit
are one and the same in all instances, especially in the Old

Testament, how do we reconcile this belief with the following verse in Jeremiah, as well as a couple of other Old Testament Scriptures?

The heart is deceitful above all things, and desperately wicked; who can know it? (Jeremiah 17:9)

That is pretty harsh, isn't it? To be honest, it sounds grim. For those folks who have not yet accepted Jesus as their Lord and Savior, that verse is true. But once born again, I promise you, our spirit is not wicked, nor deceitful. Before our new birth, our spirit is deaf to God's voice. Spiritually dead people do not long to live a lifestyle pleasing to Him. Why? Because He is not living inside them, so their hearts are dark, full of sin, and desperately wicked. But the miraculous new birth changes all of that. We are justified and reconciled to Him, literally made in His image. Glory to God! Spirits made in the image of the Almighty are neither deceitful nor wicked.

We need to get in the Word to see what it actually says, because we at times believe things that are not so. We must let the Word do the talking; in other words, keep it in context. Let me give you an example in the natural realm; sometimes it is easier to see spiritual truths there. If I were to ask you to give me the heart of a watermelon, it would be the center part, the best part, the part with no seeds. The heart is the center of the melon. In the same way, our heart is almost always—in the Old Testament and sometimes even in the New Testament—the center of our soulish area. The heart is the center of the intellect, the mind, and the emotions.

If our spirits are God-indwelt and in right standing with Him, and our hearts are the center of our spirit, how in the world can our hearts be wicked? Never, ever is there a word spoken against the born-again spirit. Not so with the heart.

There are some pretty tough things said about the heart in the Bible. Every attitude, every appetite, every issue of our life will be interpreted through the soulish area, meaning the heart in most instances. That is why we must renew our minds and save our souls by the Word of God.

Scripture states that out of a good heart, good things come to pass, and out of a bad heart, bad things come to pass. The heart and the spirit cannot be one and the same in all instances. Our born-again spirit is after God. It is clean and pure. That is where the Holy Spirit resides—inside our born-again spirit. Do you want to tell me that the heart of our spirit is deceptive? I don't think so! Think about it.

Keep in mind we are not talking about the physical heart that pumps blood throughout our body. That is where people got so confused when doctors began performing heart transplants years ago. Boy, did we hear some wild tales. Sally is not Sally anymore because she now has Sue's heart," it was said. How does Sally know what she is thinking, it could be one of Sue's thoughts. And what if Sue loved Tom and Sally is married to Dick? Who is Dick married to now? Listen, we laugh now about it, but major controversy in theological circles erupted from such questions. I am telling you, we were dumb and dumber—Jesus help us.

Keep your heart with all diligence, for out of it spring the issues of life (Proverbs 4:23).

That is not to say, "Do not have a heart transplant." I am going to show you how protecting our hearts and renewing our hearts and minds are hitting at the same thing. As a person thinks in his or her heart, so is that person (see Prov. 23:7). In other words, if someone thinks a certain way, that is the way that person really is. Well, what part does thinking come from? It comes from the mind, in the soulish part of our being. The heart does think, and many of our thought processes take place in the heart. Every action we perform outwardly is a result of our heart (soulish area) and its condition. That is bad news if our heart has problems.

Humans are made up of three components: spirit, soul, and body. We are a spirit; we have a soul; and we live in a body. When we die, we leave the body, but we are still alive. Our spirit is of God, born of God, made in the image of God. Our soul is our mind, will, and emotions. That is the part of us that we are instructed to renew by the Word of God. If we desire to think God's thoughts, we have to learn to think differently. That process is called renewing the mind.

The Bible says that the Word of God is able to save the soul, make it line up with the Word of God. This is so we can walk in victory in our soulish area and allow our spirit to get in agreement with the Word of God, thus conquering the flesh, which is always at enmity with the spirit.

Many times when the Bible speaks of the heart, it is talking about the soulish area. Let's look at some Scriptures that refer to this:

> *You should know in your **heart** that as a man chastens his son, so the Lord your God chastens you* (Deuteronomy 8:5).

> *And it happened, as she continued praying before the Lord, that Eli watched her mouth. Now Hannah spoke in her **heart**; only her lips moved, but her voice was not heard. Therefore Eli thought she was drunk* (1 Samuel 1:12-13).

> *Let the words of my mouth and the meditation of my **heart** be acceptable in Your sight, O Lord, my strength and my Redeemer* (Psalm 19:14).

> *For assuredly, I say to you, whoever says to this mountain, "Be removed and be cast into the sea," and does not doubt in his **heart**, but believes that those things he says will be done, he will have whatever he says* (Mark 11:23).

> *But immediately, when Jesus perceived in His **spirit** that they reasoned thus within themselves, He said to them, "Why do you reason about these things in your **hearts**?"* (Mark 2:8).

> *Your word have I hidden in my **heart**, that I might not sin against You* (Psalm 119:11).

*Do not let them not depart from your eyes; keep them in the midst of your **heart** (Proverbs 4:21).*

*But Mary kept all these things and pondered them in her **heart** (Luke 2:19).*

*That if you confess with your mouth the Lord Jesus and believe in your **heart** that God has raised Him from the dead, you will be saved (Romans 10:9).*

That is only a few of the heart- and soul-related Scripture verses. The following are more for you to read: Exodus 4:14,21; Deuteronomy 6:5; First Chronicles 22:19; Second Chronicles 6:7; Psalm 119:36; Proverbs 12:25; Isaiah 57:15; Luke 24:32; John 14:1; and Romans 10:1.

AN IMPURE HEART

An impure heart can corrupt our thoughts, not to mention our feelings, our words, and our actions. Knowing this can change our lives forever! When we get this, then we can apply the Blood of Jesus as priests to those who have walked away from God. Then watch God work!

As priests of God, we have a right to apply the Blood to certain situations and certain people, especially those in our household and family. We can apply the Blood to somebody's heart (in the Spirit realm) and affect the person's mind, will, and emotions. By allowing the Blood of Jesus in, to flow through and upon them, we can break away the blinders from their soulish eyes so they can have clearer vision and understanding of the things of God.

We may have some disagreement about dealing with the will of a person, but I want you to think about something. No one in their right mind chooses to go to hell. They are deceived and blinded; satan has captured them against their will, meaning they did not deliberately choose hell for their lives and their eternal future.

No one sets out to end up in captivity. We walk on our path thinking we are making sound decisions for our lives. Before we came to the Lord, you and I were held captive by deception and blindness as well. As unregenerate people, our hearts were perverted toward God and His ways of living uprightly.

After our new birth and after some learning and understanding of the Word of God, we realize it is our choices that guide our lives. But there are multitudes who know nothing about God or how He desires to flood their lives with goodness! There are many who are absolutely drawn to sin. They cannot see sin the way God sees it because their eyes are blinded by the enemy of their soul.

When we talk about the heart, we're talking about that part of each of us that was not brought immediately under the redemption of the Blood of Jesus. It does not obtain the benefits of this redemption until we apply the Blood, do what Romans 12:1-2 talks about, and start renewing our soulish areas with His Word so we can think the thoughts of God. Jeremiah 17:9 says that our hearts are desperately wicked that no one can know it. He says our hearts are deceitful. Guess who is deceived? Us! We go around thinking how wonderful and good we are. About the time we think we have it together, we are deceived. Our spirits can be righteous in the sight of God, but our hearts can be wicked and deceitful.

Could it be that every shortcoming and failure that you and I have had is a result of an area of our heart that has not been dealt with by the Blood of Jesus? Yes, it could. Not because the Blood of Jesus cannot soak into every crevice of our heart and cleanse us, but because the Lord will not impose Himself on us. He will not come in without an open invitation to all areas of our heart.

Think about a few people you know who are born again, but not serving God. We're not talking about the lost now, but members of the Body of Christ. They came to the Lord Jesus, but we cannot find them now. They are not in church anywhere. They used to be on fire for the things of God, but now they're cold, and it seems as if their hearts have become hard. Their spirits are not hard, but their hearts, their souls are. We all know folks who go around the same mountain a thousand times.

Mamas and daddies are grieved about their children who have walked away from God. They are not praying or reading God's precious Words of instruction. We can beg them to come back, or threaten them with the prospect of hell if they do not straighten up. We've tried everything we can think of, but these people just keep on running the other way just as fast as they can, into all kinds of sin.

We get torn up because they have not heard a word we have said. We cry, we intercede, we wonder what's going on.

We cannot understand the problem, because we know they know better. Nothing seems to faze them. But there is something that God has already accomplished that will help us to set them free. Praise God forevermore. Thank Him for the Blood of the Lamb.

A PURE HEART

*Blessed are the **pure in heart**, for they shall see God* (Matthew 5:8).

*A good man out of the good treasure of his **heart** brings forth good things, and an evil man out of the evil treasure brings forth evil things* (Matthew 12:35).

If the pure in heart are the only ones to see God, then it seems to me that something needs to be done at the heart level. We are not going to change these people just by our prayers; we also have to deal with their heart. I remind you that the Bible says that the heart is desperately wicked. As a matter of fact, Scripture states that there is warfare at the heart level. The apostle Paul dealt with this very issue. He wanted to do one thing, but he ended up doing another. He wanted to do good, but found himself doing just the opposite. In essence he says, "You know I really want to serve God, but there is another side of me that does not want to serve Him at all" (see Rom. 7:14-17).

I know what it's like to be saved and still be divided. Are you honest enough to admit that very same thing? I am telling you, it is a heart problem. But, thank God, there is hope for our hearts. I want to show you why that is; and then I want to show you what we can do about it as kings and priests unto God, walking in Kingdom authority, and living effectually for and in the Kingdom of God. Hallelujah!

CHAPTER 6

THOROUGHLY CLEANSED

In the previous chapters, I shared that the reason many times we fall back into trouble and fail to maintain victory after repenting is because we have not washed ourselves with the Blood of the Lamb and allowed cleansing and healing to take place deep within us. It has been very common in the Church to believe that once people are saved they are okay and that is all there is. Many times we stay with them until they accept the Lord Jesus, but then basically abandon them after that, thinking that because now they are saved, they are fine. Yet we turn up our noses at their behavior as if some magical something will change their actions overnight! Sadly, sometimes we have thought, *Get with the program, guys. Get your act together.*

We have failed to remember they are but babies in the Kingdom of God. The saints have not taught them about the power of the Blood of Jesus, nor have we nurtured them as babies. None of us were born spiritual giants. We were all born as babies into the Kingdom of God, ignorant concerning how it works. Without teaching, everyone remains an infant in spiritual things. We have been casting babies out into a world that is devouring these little ones in Christ. We must give people time to be cleansed and healed. We must tell them about the power, authority, and victory available to them.

We are called to walk in His image, but when sin enters our lives, we become defiled. Amazingly, Jesus is coming back for a glorious, victorious Church that has overcome the trials of life. Can we ever get there? We sure can. Jesus has paid for everything we need to walk in this glorious state. The provision of the Blood is the powerhouse of God. The Blood was the ransom—the price paid for eternal life. In fact, the higher life is where He wants us, so we have all of the assistance of Heaven. Life in Jesus is just too good! Hallelujah! Let's look at another Scripture.

> *Then He came to Simon Peter. And Peter said to Him, "Lord, are You washing my feet?" Jesus answered and said to him, "What I am doing you do not understand now, but you will know after this." Peter said to Him, "You shall never wash my feet!" Jesus answered him, "If I do not wash you, you have no part with Me." Simon Peter said to Him, "Lord, not my feet only, but also my hands and my head!" Jesus said to him, "He who is bathed*

*needs only to wash his feet, but is completely clean;
and you are clean, but not all of you." For He knew
who would betray Him; therefore He said, "You are
not all clean"* (John 13:6-11).

Let's put this whole thing in perspective again. Remember
that we are talking about how to get past those besetting sins
and the constant yo-yo effect of being pulled and dragged by
things we cannot seem to overcome. We haul these things
around with us all of our lives, and then, in a moment of
weakness, wham! They pull us down completely, and we
find ourselves bottomed out in the pit.

I've got good news, though—this can be overcome. We
can walk free of it through the Blood of the Lord Jesus. That,
my friend, is shouting ground. Those verses in John 13 are
not just Scriptures on humility or about the heart of a servant. There is more revelation to this than humility.

DAILY DEFILEMENT

Jesus told Peter, *"you are clean, but not all of you"* (see John
13:10-11). Now let me ask you, who is Jesus talking about?
Most of us would blurt out, "Oh, He is talking about Judas.
He is the one who is not clean." Theologically, people agree
that Judas is the one He is talking about. But, if that is
true, and He is talking about Judas here, why is Jesus washing Peter's feet? Why is He not washing Judas? Jesus said
Peter was clean and yet He was washing Peter's feet. Could
Jesus possibly be saying that Peter had been defiled by being
around Judas?

All they needed was a little spot bath. Country folks call it a "spit bath." If you are not from the country, you probably do not have any idea what I am talking about. It is not a complete bath, just a little touchup where we hit the highs and lows. Jesus was simply saying to Peter, "I do not need to wash you all over, but there are certain places that need to be taken care of" (see John 13:10-11).

The same is true for us even today. We're already saved, already scrubbed in the Blood of the Lamb, so we do not need another bath. But, every day we become defiled by the evil world around us, and we have to wash certain things that have come in contact with that filth. There are natural areas that need constant, daily cleansing. But just as in the natural realm, there are spiritual things we should wash every day, because spiritual areas also need that same attention.

The same principle is found in Ephesians 6 where Paul talks about putting on the armor of God. He was not talking about throwing things on their heads and wrapping things around their bodies. They were not tying the Word of God on their hands or anything like that. The armor is spiritual, and it was a spiritual situation like the foot-washing Peter received from Jesus. Every area of our being needs cleansing by the Blood of Jesus, just as our natural body needs cleansing.

I used the illustration that in the natural we are born once and must continue to wash the rest of our days. Knowing that the natural is a picture of the spirit world, why is it we get born again and we think that's enough of the Blood to last the rest of our days without constantly being aware of its power and application? Why haven't we continued to wash ourselves daily with the Blood of Jesus? There are power shortages in our lives because we have been dirty, wounded, common, and stained and have failed to apply the Blood of the Lamb.

Let's be honest. We have pulled wrong people to our bosom. As the saying goes, we have gone to bed with the dogs and have gotten up with fleas. We have embraced the world and people who have no desire for us to walk uprightly.

WORDS ARE A SPIRITUAL FORCE

There are certain areas that need to be cleansed continually—particular areas that will determine whether we walk in victory or not. Our mouth is one of them. When I was growing up and I said a "dirty" word, my mother had a way of dealing with it—with a bar of soap. Do you know what I am talking about? Our mouths can be defiled spiritually as well.

The words we speak are extremely important. They literally set our destiny and the goals we will ultimately reach—good or bad. We have to wake up, stop that mess, and align our words with the Word of God, because all the junk that oozes out of our mouths is causing defeat in our lives. We must quit running our mouths, playing games, and talking about things of the world with laughter when they are abominations to God.

Those who know I am a pastor are watchful of what they say around me. They try to talk faith to me. But I hear things nonetheless, and some of it grieves me. I hear people laughing and saying, "If I didn't have to be here and Pastor wasn't around, I would be doing this and that." That kind of stuff is not funny to me. They are basically coming to church for show. They are not walking out the high calling in Christ Jesus.

People, pastors included, do not save us, make us, or break us. We write our own destiny. We must learn to watch what we say because there is great power in our speech. In addition, Jesus Himself said that our words are an accurate indication of the condition of our hearts. Listening to people, it does not take very long to find out where they are spiritually.

The Bible also says that our words are a spiritual force that should be used as instruments to bring deliverance to those who are in captivity. Are our words being used in that capacity? With our speech, we should be setting people free from oppression, not putting them in bondage. In God's sight, when we gossip, we are issuing forth profanities when we should be operating in His honor. Too many people "roast" the pastor after church during lunch. Then there are those who are super holy, who call others and spread gossip under the guise of prayer. We can imagine them thinking, *Well, I'm only telling them so they can pray, aren't I?*

Too often we are deceived. We're gossiping even though we do not call it that. No, we use nicer words than that, like "sharing" and "helping." In truth, God has never asked anybody to call everybody in town and tell them everything that is going on so they can pray. Oh sure, He wants you to pray, but remember that *"love will cover a multitude of sins"* (1 Pet. 4:8).

The Bible says that Jesus cast out demons by the words of His mouth. We either flow in the power of God or we flow in the powers of the flesh. One or the other is guiding our lives. When we come into the presence of God, our lips should continue to release His awesome presence and give Him liberty to minister among the people. But too often we come to Him with defiled lips, and our praise does not go very high.

How do we defile our lips? We do that in obvious ways like when cursing and profanities come out of our mouths, but we also do it in ways that are less obvious. When we engage in ungodly conversations, gossip and cause strife, or backbite and belittle people, our mouths can no longer be considered instruments of life. This is a serious issue!

With our mouths we have destroyed people, and then we come to church and sing praises to God. Who are we fooling? We might have deceived ourselves that everything is fine, but we certainly have not fooled God. He heard every word of it and can read our minds, too! Some saints have bumper stickers on their cars: "Honk if you love Jesus." Yet when somebody honks in response to seeing the sticker, the poor, unsuspecting soul may get an unexpectedly rude piece of mind. The other driver was just responding to the bumper sticker, while the owner just happened to forget about the sticker on his car. We can just imagine the owner thinking, *Get out of my way! Can't you see I'm on the way to church to worship God?* It would be funny if it were not so true.

My friend, we are either going to flow in the power of God or we are going to move in the power of the flesh—one or the other. And we are the ones who choose our pathway every hour of every day.

It is vital that our lips remain clean. Perhaps it would be a good idea to go back to the law and review the ordinances of cleansing that had to take place before someone could participate in the sacrifices and the offerings dealing with the shedding of sacrificial blood. There was an enormous amount of cleansing that took place continually or they could not proceed further:

> *In the year that King Uzziah died, I saw the Lord sitting on a throne, high and lifted up, and the train of His robe filled the temple. Above it stood seraphim; each one had six wings: with two he covered his face, with two he covered his feet, and with two he flew. And one cried to another and said: "Holy, holy, holy is the Lord of hosts; the whole earth is full of His glory!" And the posts of the door were shaken by the voice of him who cried out, and the house was filled with smoke. So I said: "Woe is me, for I am undone! Because I am a man of **unclean lips**, and I dwell in the midst of a people of unclean lips; for my eyes have seen the King, the Lord of hosts"* (Isaiah 6:1-5).

Isaiah was a pretty good fellow, don't you think? He was a wonderful, true prophet of the Lord, but he said, *"Woe is me."* We know what happened. A seraphim came to him with a live coal off of the altar and laid it on Isaiah's mouth. In this act, his iniquity was taken away, and his sin was purged. I want you to clearly see the importance of clean lips and a clean mouth.

HEALING HANDS

What about our hands? Our hands are instruments of healing through which God can work; and they are tools to defeat the powers of darkness. Glory to God that we have such tools! Do you remember the ninth plague that befell the Egyptians under Moses' command?

> *Then the Lord said to Moses, "Stretch out your **hand** toward heaven, that there may be darkness over the land of Egypt, darkness which may even be felt." So Moses stretched out his **hand** toward heaven, and there was thick darkness in all the land of Egypt three days. They did not see one another; nor did anyone rise from his place for three days. But all the children of Israel had light in their dwellings* (Exodus 10:21-23).

Moses never said a word, he just stretched his hand toward heaven and the darkness came. And how about the battle that the children of Israel faced with Amalek?

> *And Moses said to Joshua, "Choose us some men and go out, fight with Amalek. Tomorrow I will stand on the top of the hill with the rod of God in*

*my **hand**." So Joshua did as Moses said to him, and fought with Amalek. And Moses, Aaron, and Hur went up to the top of the hill. And so it was, when Moses held up his **hand**, that Israel prevailed; and when he let down his **hand**, Amalek prevailed. But Moses' hands became heavy; so they took a stone and put it under him, and he sat on it. And Aaron and Hur supported his **hands**, one on one side, and the other on the other side; and his **hands** were steady until the going down of the sun* (Exodus 17:9-12).

There were no words involved here either, just hands. Our hands are important in the work of God, and they must not become defiled. Let's look at a Scripture in Habakkuk:

*O Lord, I have heard Your speech and was afraid; O Lord, revive Your work in the midst of the years! In the midst of the years make it known; in wrath remember mercy. God came from Teman, the Holy One from Mount Paran. Selah. His glory covered the heavens, and the earth was full of His praise. His brightness was like the light; He had rays flashing from His **hand**, and there His power was hidden* (Habakkuk 3:2-4).

There is something very interesting here that you need to notice. I looked up that verse and the words that were translated "horns coming out of his hand," and I discovered that according to Strong's Exhaustive Concordance, the horns refer to rays of light. So, *out of God's fingertips came streams of light that split the atmosphere.* Out of His hands flow rays of light, and in His hands is His power! This truth will propel us forward!

You and I are made in the likeness and the image of God, aren't we? We are commanded to lift up holy hands unto God and to lay hands on the sick. It was not just a suggestion or an option from God; we are supposed to do it. If God's power is in His hand, as it says in Habakkuk, and we are made in His image, then the power of God is released through our hands in a stream of light as well. Praise God and hallelujah! If our hands are defiled, we may still have a little of God's power in our hands, but it is like turning on a flashlight that has mud caked over the lens. Regrettably, God is unable to work through us and release His power when our hands are defiled.

How do we defile our hands? Well, everything from sexual sin to corrupt business practices and everything in between. When we cheat on our income taxes or participate in under-the-table dirty deals, we become dirty. When we habitually reach out and participate in things of the world and grab hold of things in this world's system, our hands get defiled.

Let me take it a step further. Spiritually defiled, unclean people surround us all the time. That is exactly why we are to use the Blood of Jesus daily to cleanse ourselves. Use the Blood like natural soap. In the medical profession, doctors wash their hands when they move from one patient to the next, and we should do the same in the Spirit realm.

Allow me to reveal my heart. There have been occasions when I ministered in healing lines and have laid my hands on people and literally felt the defilement attached to them. The power of God would stop, and I did not understand why. In the past, I did not know what to do, but I do now. I apply the Blood of Jesus to my hands and keep on ministering. Glory to God forevermore. God always has an answer for every dilemma we encounter. Hallelujah!

> *Who may ascend into the hill of the Lord? Or who may stand in His holy place? He who has **clean hands** and a **pure heart**, who has not lifted up his soul to an idol, nor sworn deceitfully* (Psalm 24:3-4).

We simply cannot enter into the presence of God if we do not have clean hands. When the saints are cleansed—our mouths, our hands, and our hearts washed clean by the Blood of the Lamb—we can come into His presence and worship our magnificent God. Our hands are raised in adoration to Him. Think of what is happening in the spirit dimension. Hundreds, perhaps even thousands of hands are raised toward heaven, and out of every finger light radiates and pierces the darkness, sending out beacons of light. Can we even imagine such a glorious thing? Yet, according to God's Holy Word, that is exactly what happens when we come to Him pure.

If all believers came before Him like that, can you imagine what could happen? Your church would be absolutely filled with the light of God. If multiplied thousands of churches all over the nations would grasp and act on this revelation, then the Gospel light would penetrate every dark region of the world! Evangelism would explode. I am telling you, this is real!

One time after I taught this truth, people returned to their workplace to put it to work. These people did not say anything to anyone, but inconspicuously extended their hands toward areas where there had been difficulties, believing God to bring light into their workplaces and change the atmosphere. In each incident, in every location this was done, the atmosphere immediately changed in their favor. We just do not know what power we have been given in our hands, do we?

THE POWER

Let me tell you a true story that happened to me years ago. At the close of a service one Sunday morning, I stepped down from the platform while the congregation stood to be dismissed. It was a particularly large group that day; it was a packed house. In stature, I am relatively short, so could not see the people in the back of the room. I pointed my finger and waved my hand to indicate the location of someone to whom God wanted to minister. All of a sudden—Wham! Bam! Bam! Chairs flew in every direction. I did not see what caused it and I did not know what happened. I just heard the commotion. I waited a moment to see if I could tell what happened, but then went on and dismissed the crowd when no one spoke up.

Moments after the service was over, a very large man strutted to the front of the room where I was standing and asked me pointedly, "Where did you get that power in your hands"? When I asked him what he was talking about, he said, "When you moved your hand and pointed your finger in my direction, out of your finger came a bolt of light that went through the congregation, hit me in the head, and knocked me out!"

I did not know it at the time, but, glory to God, the man was a warlock and wanted to know where I got that kind of power because he wanted it. "His name is Jesus," I exclaimed. Raise your hands, my friend, and let's cause havoc in the kingdom of darkness! Thank You, Jesus.

Interestingly, that man is not the only person who has asked me such a question. We need to be cognizant of what our actions can accomplish in the Spirit realm. I have been in church services and snapped my fingers and had people fall out as if they had been knocked down with a two-by-four. In one meeting, I raised my hands and pointed toward the congregation, and about 400 people hit the floor at the same time. I did not see it, but all of them claimed they saw fire shoot out of my hands. Praise His name. He is absolutely wonderful.

> *When they cast you down, and you say, "Exaltation will come!" Then He will save the humble person. He will even deliver one who is not innocent; yes, he will be delivered by the purity of your **hands*** (Job 22:29-30).

*When you spread out your **hands**, I will hide My eyes from you; even though you make many prayers, I will not hear. Your **hands** are full of blood* (Isaiah 1:15).

BE CAREFUL LITTLE EARS...

There is delivering power in our hands; but if they are defiled, or our hearts are not pure, our prayers are not heard. Another area of concern is our ears. It is sad when we cannot hear from God. The Bible constantly says, *"Let him that has ears, hear"* (Rev. 2:7). Everyone has some little something on the side of their head, some bigger than others. But that is not the ear He is referring to in Revelation 2:7. As a matter of fact, we can be totally deaf in the natural and still be spiritually tuned in to the things of God. It's sad when we cannot hear or see into that Spirit realm, because we will flounder. There is a children's song that has great wisdom in its words, "Be careful little ears what you hear...be careful little eyes what you see...."

I have preached this over and over again, and some are bold enough to do it, although most do not. Do not allow others to use your ears as garbage pails. Do not let them call and gossip and speak against church leadership or against your friends. Just say, "I'm sorry, but my ears are not garbage pails. I'll see you in church. Good-bye."

We need to protect our faith and our spirit. If the television broadcasts or the Internet bring all kinds of junk into our home, filled with all kinds of perversion and sin, my question is, "Why do we allow it in our homes and watch it?" Some will inevitably answer, "Well, it just came with the cable package." That package has now allowed all manner of hideous, horrid, disgusting filth to cascade into our houses like a tsunami of evil, festering, repugnant sin. And we are actually *paying* to have that mess brought into our homes. Have we forgotten about the Spirit realm and that there are things called evil spirits just waiting for the tiniest crack in the door into our lives? We need to wake up and be wise concerning both the natural and spiritual arenas.

Let's move on. Sometimes we get into things out of ignorance, but do not get stuck there. Now we'll talk about something wonderful—our privileges as priests!

CHAPTER 7

ME? A PRIEST?

Therefore, if anyone is in Christ, he is a new creation; old things have passed away; behold, all things have become new. Now all things are of God, who has reconciled us to Himself through Jesus Christ, and has given us the ministry of reconciliation (2 Corinthians 5:17-18).

Glory to God! In the spirit realm, all things become new at the moment of our new birth in the Spirit realm. That is tough to grasp. I remember when I first heard that. I used to look at my life and think, *It doesn't seem new to me.* I did not act new. As a matter of fact, not one thing appeared new to me, but actually looked worse because I did not have an understanding of spiritual things. It is our spirit that is new. It is our spirit that now responds to God. Praise Him! Our spirit, the *real self*, is no longer controlled by the devil. We have a new Master, a new King who is good and full of mercy.

Read Second Corinthians 5:18 again. God says we are ministers. We are to minister reconciliation to the world that does not yet know Him. We're to tell them, "God is not angry at you! He loves you. He wants to bless you and wants you in His household. He wants to indwell you, so He can be the Friend who sticks closer to you than a brother!" That is good news.

We are appointed, anointed, chosen by God Himself to be ministers of reconciliation. That is who we are. You and I have that ministry—every believer is a minister in the eyes of God—not just those standing behind the pulpit. We are all priests in His eyes. Let's look at a few more Scriptures that establish that truth:

> *Therefore, laying aside all malice, all deceit, hypocrisy, envy, and all evil speaking, as newborn babes, desire the pure milk of the word, that you may grow thereby, if indeed you have tasted that the Lord is gracious. Coming to Him as to a living stone, rejected indeed by men, but chosen by God and precious, you also, as living stones, are being built up a spiritual house, **a holy priesthood**, to offer up spiritual sacrifices acceptable to God through Jesus Christ* (1 Peter 2:1-5).

We are a holy priesthood. When Jesus came, He not only fulfilled that, but He fulfilled that for us. He put in order a New Covenant that is a better spiritual covenant. In verse 5 of First Peter 2, notice what the priesthood is supposed to do. We are to offer up spiritual sacrifices. We can apply the Blood of Jesus to our heart so that our hard heart of unbelief can become soft before Him. What is equally as wonderful is that we, as priests before God, can apply the Blood to our brothers and sisters in the Lord to release Him to delve into their hearts to help them. We can even act as priests and apply the Blood to those who do not know Him. God purposely built us up to be spiritual houses, a holy priesthood to offer up spiritual sacrifices acceptable to Him by Jesus Christ to reconcile people unto God.

> *But you are a chosen generation, **a royal priesthood**, a holy nation, His own special people, that you may proclaim the praises of Him who called you out of darkness into His marvelous light* (1 Peter 2:9).

The King James Version says, *"But ye are a chosen generation, a royal priesthood, an holy nation, a **peculiar** people...."* We know about being peculiar, don't we? We are quite familiar with that part, but why is it that we know more about that than being a royal priesthood. We go around saying, "We are peculiar," and some of us extend beyond the boundaries of peculiar. But the priesthood is the more important part of our character.

> *And has made us **kings and priests** to His God and Father, to Him be glory and dominion forever and ever. Amen* (Revelation 1:6).

> *And has made us **kings and priests** to our God; and we shall reign on the earth* (Revelation 5:10).

*Blessed and holy is he who has part in the first resur-rection. Over such the second death has no power, but they shall be **priests** of God and of Christ, and shall reign with Him a thousand years* (Revelation 20:6).

We are kings and we are priests—that is very clear. The King rules and reigns, and although we stand in that role when we take authority, that part of us will show forth more in the millennium and eternity when we rule and reign with King Jesus. We like having dominion. But, we've been pretty weak in our priestly role, which is where our hearts needs to be centered now. We need to be excited that we have some authority as a priest to cause people's hearts to be softened and more tender toward God. In fact, the priestly part of our responsibilities is what moves us into the kingship part.

THE PRIESTLY ROLE

Being a priest does not mean wearing a suit with our collar turned around. I know the root of that tradition, but just realize that the collar is merely a symbol that some spiritual leaders use to set themselves apart. It is perfectly fine to do that, but it does not have any spiritual connotation to it. If you want to wear a collar, wear one.

I have spent many hours researching the functions of a priest. In the Bible, the functions do not change over time. What the biblical priests did in the natural, we do now in the spirit. You are going to love this. The chief function is the care of the vessels of the sanctuary and the sacrificial duties of the altar. We can be vessels of honor or vessels of dishonor (see 2 Tim. 2:20). It certainly would not take much time to discover that people are the vessels to whom God is referring.

Only the priests may offer sacrifices of any kind (see Num. 18:5,7). The priests also give instruction in the ways and requirements of God. I am not talking about the High Priest. I am talking about priests. They are the authority regarding the law and agents of revelation to the people. Now this is great: the priests are the custodians of the medical arena and play an important part safeguarding the health of the community (see Lev. 13:15)! Did you get that? People wonder if we are to lay hands on the sick to be healed. According to the law, the priests are to be custodians of the medical arena and safeguards to the health of the community.

According to these Scriptures, we are priests unto God *now*—not when we get to Heaven, and not only if or when we ever get behind a pulpit. We are declared to be priests from the moment of our new birth to apply the Blood of Jesus. For what reason? Reconciliation of every kind. God wants us to live our lives as priests before Him, applying the Blood to bring people back in fellowship with God and soundness to their lives! Thank You, Jesus. We can get happy about that, my friend!

The Word of God calls us priests. Out of the mouths of two or three witnesses, let a thing be established (see Deut. 19:15). Priests are administrators of justice, to see that those who have been defiled are reconsecrated to the Lord. They ensure that those who have been defiled, those who are dirty, common, stained, or wounded are reconciled back to God! The world is waiting for us to take our place. Surely, there is no hope for them without us being what God has ordained us to be. They also blow the trumpets that summon the people to war or for the keeping of a feast. Priests may also bless in the name of the Lord! Are you grasping the privilege we have been given? This is who the Bible says we are.

We are born into God's Kingdom as priests, not made to become one. We must learn how to operate in this office. In the spirit realm, we are defiled when we are around people who are spiritually dead. But as priests, we can be cleansed from this defilement by the Blood. Also, we can apply the Blood to that person's hard heart so they can be reconciled to God.

A ministry of reconciliation is the ministry of priests. That is what they do; they mediate between man and God. We need people serving in their spiritual capacity as our priests. We need godly council and explanation of the Word of God. We need correction and admonition to stay on the right path. Thank God for those in the Body of Christ who have been operating in that capacity. No doubt, they have been overwhelmed with the needs of people. All of us should have been walking in our priestly responsibilities and privileges, but it was left on the shoulders of a few.

Priests were the ones who took the blood to the altar and applied it there as a holy sacrifice. We need to take advantage of the shed Blood of Jesus for our families and their deliverance. Do you know what has held people captive? My Bible tells me in Second Corinthians 4:4 that deception and blindness are the culprits, but the Blood of Jesus is well able to wash away that mess and open their eyes. You can pray for Joe Blow down the street who has been driving you bananas, covering him in the Blood of Jesus, and then watch him change and move into the things of God. All you are doing is operating in your office as a priest—and ordained of God to do so.

HEART TROUBLE

Yes, Jesus fulfilled the law. He is still the Morning and Evening Sacrifice; and He did it just for us. He fulfilled the law so that He could make it applicable to our lives. But we have to *apply* this truth. We have to *get involved* in what Jesus has accomplished for us.

Priests had to have pure hearts. Some of us have crusty old hearts, and we have to "massage" them and penetrate them with the Blood to get results. The more we apply it in faith, the softer the heart gets. Are our hearts pure, or do we have heart problems?

Let's take a look at the *five characteristics of heart trouble* and see where we measure up.

Five Characteristics of Heart Trouble

1. When people have heart trouble, they have no power over sin. In other words, these people are constantly doing the same thing over and over

again. They do not necessarily want to do anything about it in the first place. We can talk to them until we are blue in the face and it is just like talking to a tree. There are multitudes who cannot seem to help themselves. They want to, but they cannot. They try, but they never make it. They are on the edge, but never seem to make it in—flip-flopping from the Church to the darkness of worldly things. There are many in the Church who continue to go around in circles. They go round and round the mulberry bush because they are not willing to deal with their sinful behavior.

We can have a perfect heart one day, and lose it by nightfall because we get defiled. If we do not stay in the Word of God for daily instruction and keep ourselves cleansed by the Blood of the Lamb, we can go down a wrong road to former habits without much thought. We need to act like King David did after his sin with Bathsheba, "Lord, create in me a clean heart" (Ps. 51:10). The response of people who have perfect hearts is that we are saddened by our sin. We are burdened by our sin and want to be free of it. If this is you, say, "Hallelujah! I am going to be free of this thing—*today!* I have a heart problem and I need help." And thank God, we can be free.

2. Another symptom of heart trouble is whether or not we have a hunger for God and His Word and have a willingness to be doers of that Word. Do we like to apply the words of God to our personal lives, or do we just like to hear them on occasion? Most people who think like that do not attend church, but that is not necessarily true all the time. We can be sitting in church and still have heart trouble. Do we really love the Word of God? Is it really life to us? If we have spiritual heart disease, it is difficult to love God's Word.

Let me say this, too—we cannot say we love God's Word and choose to stay away from Church. That may be hard to swallow, but that is the truth. The Bible says that God's Word is medicine for whatever ails us. The Word about the Blood of the Lamb can cleanse us, heal us from our heart trouble. God is indeed our Helper and Deliverer.

3. Those of us who have heart problems most often have attitudes of unbelief and carnality. Basically, unbelief is just another form of carnality. The Bible is clear, the carnal mind does not receive anything from God. He is Spirit, and we must hear and receive from Him with the spirit. Some people attend a church service, and receive nothing from it. Then they question

everything, wondering whether it was a movement of God or not. We think in the carnal realm because we cannot keep tuned in to the things of God. Everything that takes place in the service is rationalized back to the natural realm, while we fail to understand spiritual things.

We are spirit, but most of us often allow our flesh to rule us, don't we? God's intent is that the spirit inside us—the part that is born again and made in the image of God—should rule the flesh within which it dwells.

4. People with heart problems are not givers. When I hear someone say something like, "I knew she'd get around to money. See there, preachers cannot say anything without talking about money," I know that is a carnal mind talking. God loves a cheerful giver, but these people are neither givers nor tithers. As a matter of fact, they nickel and dime God. Let's examine ourselves. Are we greedy, tending to hold on to our money, refusing to turn it loose when prompted by the Lord? Are we looking for opportunities to give, or do we cringe when offering time comes around?

5. A final symptom of someone with spiritual heart disease is a lack of hunger for God's

presence and the things of God. Because that is not where their hearts are, they are unaware of His presence. They have no earthly idea whether He is in the room or not; they are not spirit-centered. Have you ever been in a time of praise and worship and the song leaders kept singing the same song over and over again? The anointing gets on a song and if they are sensitive to the move of God's Spirit, they will stay with that song because the anointing can destroy the yokes of bondage. If the worship leaders move to a new song too soon, the anointing will lift, and it will be very obvious to those who are in the spirit.

People with spiritual heart trouble have great difficulty flowing with God because they are unable to recognize His presence when He walks in. This may come as a shocker, but He does not show up in every church service in supernatural ways because He cannot bless every church service. He is capable of all things. Rather, it has a lot to do with the hearts and attitudes of the people and whether or not there is sin in the camp.

Yes, pastors need to preach against sin, but if we are even in the least measure sensitive to God, we know when we are in sin. When we are first saved, we may not know exactly what we have done, but we will know something is wrong because something will have changed inside us. All believers have experienced that, and the more we know about His Word, the more precisely we can pinpoint our error.

TOUGH TO TACKLE

Heart problems are tough to deal with in people. If we could change people's hearts, we would have done it many years ago. We have tried every strategy. Am I right? We have tried the nice approach, we have tried the mean approach. We have screamed at them, yelled at them, and begged them to come back to God. We have talked to them about hell, wrote note after note to them: "We love you. We miss you. We want you to come back…," but they just look at us. It takes the Spirit of God to deal with people's hearts.

If left untended for any period of time, our hearts will grow hard. Scripture says, *"For as he thinks in his heart, so is he"* (Prov. 23:7). If our hearts reveal to others what kind of people we actually are, then it is apparent we are going to have to deal with people (ourselves included) at the heart level. And that, my friend, will take the power of God and the precious Blood of Jesus!

Basically, heart problems set in because we have not renewed our minds with the Word of God and cleansed our-selves daily with the Blood. In truth, we can have a clean heart this morning and not have one tonight. Sometimes we can be defiled by the world and our hearts be turned away from God and taken down a dead-end road. We desperately need the Blood of the Lamb applied to our hearts as the Morning and Evening Sacrifice.

We are talking about the things of the heart. Maybe you know people who do not respond to the things of the Lord. There is a really good chance they have heart problems. Maybe it is you. Perhaps you have difficulties. You've prayed, others have prayed and laid hands on you, yet nothing changes. Have the things of the Lord grown dim to you? Have you lost the intense interest you had in His Church and His Word? Has the excitement and fire waned from your bones?

We normally think that everyone else has changed and tend to throw the blame on them. It is time to be honest. We ought to admit it to ourselves and the Lord Jesus that we have heart problems. Look at yourself right now. It is really important to self-examine, because you do not want to become hardened to sin. If we do, believe it or not, we will become indifferent to sin and will not want to repent—and that is not a good thing.

STOP FEELING, START ACTING

You may be thinking, *I don't feel like a priest.* This position is not based on feelings. We are simply acting on something that God has already declared over us. Welcome to the Light, my friend! Come out of the darkness and into the light because *you are a priest unto God.* The devil does not want us to see this because some will believe it. And some will have the audacity to start acting like priests. The devil will shake to his core because he is fully aware that things will start happening in people's hearts—and it won't be a pretty picture for him.

The only thing satan can do is hit us a few times, try to knock us down, wear us down so we quit fighting, or try to bring depression on us. Listen, that is why we were given the full armor of God. It will quench every fiery dart of the enemy! One thing we need to remember—never give up! God has already made us more than conquerors.

It is not surprising, though, that when we begin acting like priests, the people we are praying for begin acting up, usually worse than before. The devil is trying to hang on to his control over people. He makes them lash out; but many times the arrow comes straight at us.

The Blood of Jesus brings captives out of the darkness and into the Light, but let me give you a word of caution that might save you some anguish. When you begin to walk in your role as a priest, do not go up to someone and say, "Hey stupid, I'm applying the Blood of Jesus to you in hopes of turning you around!" It is better to do this in your prayer time alone with God, and let Him work unhindered. Too many times people will fight us; and yes, they will do things they know aggravate us even though they know we are praying for them. Let's pray and let God work.

We need to come in as ministers of reconciliation and let people know that Jesus loves them and cares greatly about them and about what is going on in their lives. Yes, some of them will look at us funny, but some will respond, "Thanks, I needed to hear that!" People need to hear good news. They need to hear that their situation is not hopeless.

The priest is the one ordained to give out that Good News. It is fabulous to work hand in glove with Almighty God. What a privilege we have been given! What joy to see the lives of people turn around into victory!

We are a blessed people, my friend.

We can do this!

CHAPTER 8

BRIDGING THE GAP

Say this out loud, "Yes, I am a priest before Almighty God and my ministry is reconciliation." Doesn't that sound fabulous? Whoever you are, whatever you are doing, wherever you are, you are commissioned to reconcile back to God those people who are not walking with Him. What an honor!

Above all, we ought to be ever aware that we are ministers. If we see somebody who has a sad and lonely face with no apparent hope of life in them, we are to walk as the light of the world and introduce them to the One who can turn their lives around.

Some people think that they are only supposed to be out making a living. But we need to realize we are all ministers of reconciliation. God needs the involvement of all of His people to spread the gospel.

You might think that you are in the job you have because you are an expert in that field, but you are really there because God put you there. You did not get that job on your own. The steps of a righteous and good man are ordered by the Lord, the Scripture says in Psalm 37:23.

The Lord has already established the things that He wants us to accomplish. Hell cannot stop what God is doing in our lives if we are determined to flow with God. We are not ships lost at sea bouncing around here and there. We are on a divine mission in life, and it is not mission impossible. With man, it might be impossible, but not so when God is involved. Let me remind you, we are not doing these things with our physical strength, but with the power of God.

We should be coming toward people with our spiritual antennas up, expecting to hear God's voice. He'll tell us what each person needs to hear and how to minister to each individual. We should be planting heavenly "seeds" straight from the throne of God, knowing that He will send others to water them. We need to wake up and understand that time is so short, and we have to get our act together. But we need to be sound and whole to fulfill our potential. Do not get caught up in religion and say, "They have been looking for Jesus a long time," because we are much closer than we were. The sheer fact we've been looking so long ought to motivate us to get with the program. We are the only ministers of reconciliation God has to work through. The amazing thing is that He thinks we are sufficient. He believes we can do the job—and we can.

You might be working in a difficult environment. Do you know what that says to me? God knows what He put in you and knows you have the nature to handle it. He knows that you and you alone can go into that place and do His work completely, effectively, and successfully. Wow! Almighty God put you there because there is something special about your nature, your character, something about your attributes that you can do it when others cannot and drop out. He brought you—on purpose—into that darkness as a light, as a minister of reconciliation, because you have what it takes to plow in there and pull down the forces that have held the people in captivity. You are in contact with the pit to pull them out. He does not want to lose even one person.

We may think we would like to work with a bunch of Christians, but let me tell you, if they are not walking submissively to God and under the cleansing power of the Blood of Jesus, it can be very disappointing. Christians who do not walk under the Blood of the Lamb get religious, pious, and their hearts are so hardened that they become unteachable. There's nothing like dealing with a religious spirit. They will tell you that they are washed in the Blood and have received their prayer language—but some of them can be backbiters.

What a God we have! Take advantage of the Blood of Jesus for your families. Men of the Church must learn the value of pleading the Blood over their household. Men are the priests of their homes as well as priests unto God. Single women, and married women if their husbands do not assume their priestly roles, should not get discouraged. They can still apply the Blood to their homes and families and get the same results and have the same benefits—after all, they are priests according to the Word of God.

What a difference can be made when you actually do this. Children can be set free and come back to God. In these years that are in front of you, you are going to need to know what I am teaching you now, because we are quickly moving into very perilous times. Your families are depending on you.

People who are caught in sin are blinded to truth, and we have been ordained of God to take the Blood of Jesus and clear out that blindness, to shed the scales from their eyes. Somebody has to do it—who else will do it other than God's people?

RECONCILIATION

What is reconciliation? We've talked around it, but now consider this wonderful definition: *Reconciliation is the process by which God and man are brought together again.* The Bible teaches that God and man are alienated from each other because of God's holiness and man's sinfulness. That is it in a nutshell. God is there, we are here. Somebody had to bridge the gap. We could not go to Him, so He came to us through our Lord Jesus Christ. Jesus came down to our level—tempted of every sin, well-acquainted with our infirmities and weaknesses—for the sole purpose of raising us up to live with Him. Praise God forevermore!

Some of us get to thinking, *Poor, pitiful me,* when in truth God came after us. He knows us so well, and yet loved us enough to send the Love of His Heart as our personal Sacrifice. He chose you and He chose me, and thought we were well worth the cost. This is too fabulous to believe! Even if we have made a mess of our lives, we are still chosen of God. That is what reconciliation is all about.

I do not fully understand how reconciliation works or how He does it. But, I sure am glad He does it. In the natural, I do not understand how lights work, I just flip a switch and they are supposed to come on. I do not know how my car works. I just put in gas, turn the key, and off I go, right? I do not have to identify every wire or comprehend every gizmo under the hood! I leave that to the mechanics and electricians. I just trust that whoever developed that thing knew what they were doing.

Why can't we trust God that way? Why can't we, at face value, trust that whoever wrote the Bible knew what He was doing? His name is the Holy Ghost—hallelujah—and the Author of this Book lives inside us. Let's just trust Him, shall we? Why do we stumble with that? Let's just believe what He said and get on with the program of being what God says we can be. This whole concept of reconciliation can be life-transforming, if we grab it.

Although God loves the sinner, it is impossible for Him not to judge the sin that we have committed. God took the initiative in reconciliation. We did not work this plan out. Simply put, He wanted us and came to get us. Scripture says that while we were still sinners and enemies, Christ died for us (see Rom. 5:6-10). That is amazing to me. I can imagine

Jesus saying, "Yes, I see the mess your life is in, but I've come to get you while in the mess so that I can get you out of the mess."

We cannot clean up ourselves, but, oh how hard we have tried. It takes the Spirit of God to do that. The plan of reconciliation is already in place on our behalf. All believers are ministers. That is a separate group from the fivefold ministry, those who have been licensed and ordained. When someone says, "Will all of the ministers stand up," every believer should stand to their feet. Praise God! Until we recognize who we really are, we will be ineffective in the Kingdom of God. We have had this thing all messed up—it is Jesus and Jesus alone. It has nothing to do with us. It was His plan from the beginning.

WALKING AS A MINISTER OF RECONCILIATION

There are so many Christians who desperately need to be set free. A lot of times, we are in bondage and do not know it, funny as it may seem. It is evident, though. We attend church, but we are not doing the things we should be doing for the Kingdom of God. We have too many benchwarmers, too many people who never do a thing to help anybody. They walk in on Sunday morning and leave. Period. I believe they think that church has nothing to do with life. It is just a ritual, something they do on Sunday.

It is not only our privilege, but our responsibility to walk the steps of a minister of reconciliation. Amazing as it sounds, God needs us. He has chosen to work His plan through us. This is part of the reason why we are left on earth after we are born again. We are the hands of Jesus, the mouth of Jesus, and the feet of Jesus. The Blood of the Lamb has brought us into this ministry, and this is the reason that we can be effective in the calling He has placed on our lives.

Sometimes it seems as if some churches do not care that the world is going to hell. Some are self-centered, pious "country clubs" with social and dining activities, rather than places of worship with Holy Spirit-inspired messages. That grieves the heart of our Father. He never has stayed behind the stained-glass windows. He likes to be out on the high-ways and byways giving people opportunities to come into His house.

So many people are absolutely hopeless because the world has nothing to offer. But we can tell people the Good News, "Your life can be different. Jesus knows you and truly does care for you." What a great message of life He has for a dying world. I am telling you the truth, the world is starved to hear that message.

In fact, those of us who are born again do not have a right to stay silent about Jesus Christ and what He has done for us. I believe we will give an account for keeping salvation to ourselves and holding it when it was given to us freely to share. We cannot keep quiet about our salvation when our neighbor is going to split the gates of hell wide open. I believe there will be a day of reckoning. There is a judgment seat, and we will have to answer for what we have done or not done with this so great a salvation. We may not be professional theologians, but we are vessels the Lord can use to touch the lives of others. We can give our testimony.

You may find yourself in this place today, knowing that you are not walking as a minister of reconciliation. In fact, you may not even like people. You just want them to leave you alone. If that's you, the Blood needs to be applied to your heart.

We were not saved just to sit in church on Sunday and disregard the needs of people or the situations they are facing Monday through Saturday. The entire point of the ministry of reconciliation is love, love, love. People will know that we are Christians when we show forth the love of Christ.

Many in the Church are sick simply because they are not walking in love with other people. Oh, they claim to know how to do everything, but in their hearts they are not walking in love. We have to understand this simple truth. This is our calling, to walk in love. Applying the Blood of Jesus to our hearts helps us do that. And so much more. And this is my prayer for you:

Father, in the name of Jesus, I ask You to deal with the heart of every person who reads this book. As a priest before You, I apply the precious Blood of Jesus to the deep places of each heart. May the Blood strip away the hardness, blindness, and lies that have kept them from walking the high life by Your side. May You give them a boldness to be vocal about Your goodness toward mankind. May the Blood deal with every heart problem that has hindered and held them captive and kept them from completing Your plans and purposes for them. Enable them to walk as the light of Your Gospel in the midst of this dark world; and give a deeper compassion to reach out for those still chained to that darkness. May the Blood of Jesus saturate them. Give them ears to hear, eyes to see, a mouth to be used for Your glory, feet ready to go where Your Spirit leads, and hands to be extended to bring deliverance to the captives. I thank You, Lord. I welcome Your work in the hearts of these precious people. I know it will change them. I give You glory and praise in Jesus' name. Amen.

CHAPTER 9

SIN VERSUS INIQUITY

This is the covenant that I will make with them after those days, says the Lord: I will put My laws into their hearts, and in their minds I will write them," then He adds, "Their sins and their lawless deeds I will remember no more" (Hebrews 10:16-17).

How is He going to put the law, the Word, into our hearts? Remember, we are talking about the heart as the center of our soulish area. As we renew our mind with the Word of God, then our soul is saved by the engrafted Word, and God will write the Word *on* our hearts. When we finally get our mind and spirit working together, we are a powerful force for God's agenda.

When the miraculous new birth takes place in each of us, God's methods and instructions do not instantly appear in our hearts. It certainly would be wonderful to immediately know the ways of God, but we do not. He said, "I will put My law in minds, and write it on their hearts" (see Jer. 31:33). That says to me that if we will abide under the power of the Blood of Jesus, if we will let the Blood do its work in our hearts, then God will imprint His laws so that His words become a part of us and regulate us from the inside.

Can you imagine such a thing? Isn't that absolutely wonderful? That no matter in what situation we find ourselves, bless God, we will automatically think the thoughts of God No matter what happens to us, our hearts will instinctively respond toward someone according to the ways of God. Just that alone will save us from a multitude of problems and subsequent anguish.

Knowing that our cardinal law is love, is there anyone who would not want to have a loving heart toward everybody? I know in myself, that when I begin to feel something rise up within me against someone, I am disturbed that I feel that way because I hate it. I want to walk in love. I do not like harboring things in my heart because it really bothers me. I literally fight tooth and nail to block access of any detrimental feelings into my heart.

This is something that God Himself wants to do for us. This is not some far-fetched something, but His plan from the beginning. *"This is the covenant I will make with them after those days"* (Heb. 10:16). He is talking about the days after we allow the Blood to do its work in our hearts and lives. As we apply the Blood, walk under the Blood, believe the Blood, and as we gain the knowledge of the reality of the Blood and allow it to penetrate us, God makes our hearts soft and pliable and responsive to Him so we can think from a heavenly perspective. What a mighty God we serve, love, and hold dear! Thinking the thoughts of God—what a thrill. This is not beyond reach for any believer. This has been the plan of God for each one of His children from the beginning.

Hebrews 10:16-17 tells us that when we apply the Blood, believe in the Blood, and walk under the covering of the Blood, then there is no remembrance of sins or iniquities. I do not want to remember my sins. It thrills me to know that Almighty God has completely forgotten about them. To tell you the truth, I have no intention of reminding Him of them.

There are, however, plenty of people who will remind us and God about our sins and shortcomings, I assure you. As a matter of fact, it's unwise to come into the Holy of Holies, into the presence of the Most High God, with a "garbage pail" mouth full of gossip and slander about His sons and daughters and dump it at His feet. We might be talking about Sally and Joe, but if they are born again and covered with the Blood of Jesus, they belong to Him even if they are not acting like it.

We have all done that at one time or another. We tend to judge ourselves on our good intentions, but scrutinize others in detail by their actions. We often demand virtues in others that we do not practice ourselves. Let's use the same standard for others as we use on ourselves, shall we?

When we come to Him talking about others, something normally gets stirred up and He says, "Let's talk about you.

Let's look at the log in your own eye and deal with that first" (see Matt. 7:3-5). Ouch. I do not know about you, but I'd prefer to avoid that situation. I would much rather have Him see me garbed in glory robes, washed white by the Blood, and radiating the Lord Jesus Christ.

DIFFERENT OR THE SAME?

Let me back up a minute. Look at the Scripture passage again. Because they are mentioned separately, are sins and iniquities different?

> *This is the covenant that I will make with them after those days, saith the Lord, I will put my laws into their hearts, and in their minds will I write them; and their **sins** and **iniquities** will I remember no more* (Hebrews 10:16-17 KJV).

> *Who has believed our report? And to whom has the arm of the Lord been revealed? For He shall grow up before Him as a tender plant, and as a root out of dry ground. He has no form or comeliness; and when we see Him, there is no beauty that we should desire Him. He is despised and rejected by men, a Man of sorrows and acquainted with grief. And we hid, as it were, our faces from Him; He was despised, and we did not esteem Him. Surely He has borne our griefs and carried our sorrows; yet we esteemed Him stricken, smitten by God, and afflicted. But He was wounded for our **transgressions**, He was*

*bruised for our **iniquities**; the chastisement for our peace was upon Him, and by His stripes we are healed* (Isaiah 53:1-5).

Let's go into this a little bit more so we can understand it. We know that the Scripture in Isaiah is speaking of the Lord Jesus. There is a distinct difference between sin (or transgressions) and iniquities, but most of the Church is not aware of it. Without knowledge that Jesus took care of all of it, we are hindered from being who God really wants us to be.

The word *transgression* means sin. Jesus was wounded for our sin, the thing we do that is contrary to God's Word. He dealt with sin; but as wonderful as that is, that in itself would not be enough for us—because we keep sinning. What is it that keeps us doing the same dumb thing over and over? That, my friend, is iniquity. Isaiah saw that Jesus not only paid the price to free people from sin, but also from what keeps us sinning. By the Blood of the Lamb, we can cut off that sin at the root! Praise God. There is hope for our hearts, which can be made as white as snow by His exceptional grace of love shown in the sacrifice of Jesus.

We can know Jesus is bigger than our sin problem, but if we do not know we *can* go or *how* to go to the *root* of that nature and how to eradicate our sin nature, we go round and round the mulberry bush. We commit the act, and cry, and repent, and cry, and repent. We tell ourselves, "I am not going to do that again," but by morning we have already eaten those words and repented again.

BLOOD-COVERED POWER

Listen, all believers have the same problem—we sin. We all make mistakes. Our lives can certainly be a mess. We can even be born-again, Spirit-filled messes when we have not understood the great work He accomplished for us on the Cross and through the Resurrection over death. From time to time, we have all felt empty and void because we have been defiled by past sin. We have been forgiven all right, but have remained wounded, stained, dirty, and common. Self-help groups and do-it-yourself improvement books may address symptoms, but do not solve our problems. The Blood of the Lamb is stronger and more powerful than any problem we have, inside or out.

The more we understand what privileges and authority have been given to us as priests before God, the more victory we will experience in life. It is called the Morning and Evening Sacrifice. Over time, the thing that has been our downfall will forever come crumbling at our feet in defeat. This is a key to victorious living, not only for ourselves but for others to whom we apply the Blood.

Isaiah says that Jesus was wounded for the sins in our lives and was bruised for our iniquity. He took bruises for our iniquity—our sin nature—so that we might be entirely free. See, it is one thing to have sins forgiven; it's quite another thing to have the root of sin cut out and walk free of sin's control. Hallelujah! That thing that haunts us in the night hours and aborts in shame our praise to God can fall to its knees in submission under the power of the Blood of the High Priest of our profession.

We cannot do this on our own, but we can do it by faith in God's Word. We cannot break the power of sin or iniquity, but the Blood that speaks of better things than Abel's blood can shatter it. Praise God forevermore. Our faith in God and His graces of provision, including that of our priestly mantle, activates this truth.

In life, Christians can have drug and alcohol problems, among other things. Yes, we can. Do not be too quick to judge, though. Most are brokenhearted about it and would do anything to stop it, but they do not know how to get out from under the bondage and walk away. Those addictions are escape mechanisms from deep hurt. All of us need to learn how to operate in God's Kingdom once we are born again. We desperately need compassionate teachers and pastors who teach the way to freedom. Do not criticize; too many are yet in chains. We were all in bondage at one time.

Perhaps we might have problems with our children or our marriage. What about temper and attitude? Some of us have gone around in circles for years and years. We have screamed and yelled, and cried, repented, and then did the same dumb thing again.

We have wanted God to do it for us, never realizing that He has *already* done it for us. Do we really understand that? The work has been complete for thousands of years, all wrapped up in the Blood of the Lamb. By faith, we enter into the blessings of God; and we must labor to enter into the rest of those blessings (Heb. 4:1-11). We experience God by faith to the measure we can broaden ourselves to believe His provisions.

How critical it is to be part of a Word church—a church that teaches the Word accurately. We cannot just hear about the new birth every week. I mean, that's great for the sinner, but the saints starve to gain dimensions of faith to cover the many areas of life. Certainly, the new birth is the most important area of salvation, but it is not the only area. God sent Jesus so that we could have victory in every area: health, protection, prosperity, family, and any sort of problem.

FROM GLORY TO GLORY

We should be climbing from glory to glory, ever more closely conformed and aligned to the Lord Jesus Christ. We should look like Him, act like Him, pray like Him, constantly gaining all of the victories that we need for ourselves and others. We build line upon line, precept upon precept (2 Cor. 3:10; Isaiah 28:10). But His Word will only work in those who believe His Word will work; it doesn't automatically happen simply because we belong to Him. That would be great if it were that way, but it is not. We are getting back to the subject of free will; we can walk in God as much as we want to. Here again, we can—should—put on our priestly robes and apply the Blood to the hearts of people. Who in their right mind does not want success in all that they do? No one.

Just because someone dies and splits hell's gates wide open does not mean that Jesus did not want that person in Heaven. He desires *all* to repent and come to the knowledge of the truth (see 1 Tim. 2:3-4). That person either did not know the provision of forgiveness or was deceived and rejected it. The Blood of the Lamb can be applied to a person's eyes, mind, and heart daily. The Blood will remove the root of their problem, if we stay with it, determined to pray. Do not do it just one time and then say, "It didn't work." *The Word works and it works every time. The Blood works and it works every time.*

That's what I see so often in the Church. Have you ever prayed for somebody and it is like you were praying for a dead tree? Over a period of time we just give up and say, "Forget it, if they want to go to hell, let 'em go! My hands are clean." Not so, my friend. Do not turn loose of the power of God in your life or in anybody else's life. We have all been frustrated with people, although we do not like to admit it. It is not very spiritual, is it? We must remember that we are dealing with blinded minds, hardened hearts, and sometimes even evil spirits. People are never our problem, although they appear to be so. There is no situation that the Blood cannot resolve, no wound the Blood cannot heal, no stain the Blood cannot remove.

Stay with it, and then get ready for the thrill of your life.

CHAPTER 10

TOO HARD FOR GOD?

The Lord says in Ezekiel 36:26, "I will give you a new heart and put a new spirit within you; I will take the heart of stone out of your flesh and give you a heart of flesh." A heart of flesh is a heart that is soft; one that is pliable in God's hands. What a great promise! That is the will of our Father that our stony hearts be crumbled and replaced with ones that respond to His voice. That is so good, I just want to shout! I know shouting makes a lot of people nervous, but it does not bother me at all. God delivered me out of the pit, not just some little hole in the ground. I was way below ground level when God showed me the light of the escape route. It came through the Word of God, and I am so grateful for His work in my life. I will never be able to thank Him enough for the mercy and kindness He has extended toward me.

He really does want our hearts to hear Him, and hear Him clearly. Therefore, I understand that excitement completely when from the depths of their hearts people begin to praise the Almighty.

> *Being confident of this very thing, that He which hath begun a good work in you will **perform** it until the day of Jesus Christ* (Philippians 1:6 KJV).

My Bible has a center reference column and lists *complete* as a substitute for the word "perform." So, *He who has begun a good work in us will complete it.* Isn't that glorious? But He does not just complete it on His own; He requires our participation. He completes it as we release our faith in the area that needs completion, as we continue to trust Him and stay pressed in to Him. We cannot expect God to start a work in us and then while we live like idiots the work gets completed. We have to guard not only what He's doing in our lives, but also what He has already accomplished in us.

Some days life is smooth and easy. But when the crises of life come, we will either sink or swim depending on what we believe about God. Do we believe He will complete the work that He has begun in us, and do we believe He will not forsake us? If we believe that, we will begin to speak it.

It is also true that our families get tuned in to our nature, habits, and reactions. They know how to "read" us, so to speak. Sometimes, they have to walk on egg shells because they are concerned we are going to unleash our mouth on them. One day we bless them and the next day we curse them. We act like we are serving God, being so holy, doing things at church—but in reality, our family is afraid of us. Something is terribly wrong with that.

Listen, people are peculiar. They want us to love God, but do not really want us to love Him more than they do because they think it makes them look bad, or it makes them feel bad and often act as if they are not growing in the things of God. When we start applying the Blood of Jesus to our lives morning and evening, we need to keep it between ourselves and God for a while. Let those deep changes of our heart bubble to the surface and affect our behavior for them to see. While they might be skeptical at first, before long they will see the glorious changes that God is working in our lives. Oh yes, we can change. If God can change me, He surely can change you!

Ah, Lord God! Behold, You have made the heavens and the earth by Your great power and outstretched arm. **There is nothing too hard for You.** *..."Behold, I am the Lord, the God of all flesh.* **Is there anything too hard for Me?**" (Jeremiah 32:17,27)

Is there anything too hard for our God? Absolutely not. I will tell you right now, it is too hard for you and it is too hard for me, but nothing is impossible for Him. He can touch us way down at the deepest levels, in the remote chasms, in the dark places of our hearts, and He knows exactly what needs to be done in every area of our lives. He is constantly working in us to perform what He has started in us. The "Greater One" lives in us. If we can believe that, and I mean sincerely believe that, then it becomes a huge revelation in itself. Then we can begin to see our entire nature change.

NEW NATURE VS. OLD NATURE

There is something that really bothers me within the church body. From a platform in the front of a church, I can see a lot, including people and their actions that reflect their character. Some continually look at their watch—not conspicuously, of course. They are the ones who are so anxious to get out of church, yet many times, they are the ones who have the biggest problems. Does that make sense? I see people who do not care whether their nature is ever changed for the better; people who are perfectly satisfied with their roughness and gruffness, and their tepid dedication. Some are unconcerned if they offend everyone in their path or if they act like bullies. That upsets me!

It is disheartening to me when I hurt someone or offend some precious person. I certainly do not mean to do it, but there it is...the damage of my old nature raising its ugly head. When my life does not show forth the glory of the Lord, it hurts me. Appalled at my own actions, I'm grieved because I've not been the witness that Jesus so needed me to be. You may feel the same way; we both want to have God's heart and shine forth His goodness. We want to respond as He would, not as an unregenerate person. He did not belittle people, yell at them, or gossip about their actions to others. He just loved them. Surely He confronted people, but that too was out of love.

This revelation is so exciting to me. To think I can be completely free, not only from sin, but its defilement and its power, is almost beyond my comprehension.

Let's put on our priestly garments, come before God boldly as He has instructed us, and apply the Blood, morning and evening, with the words of our mouth to our own heart and the hearts of others. It will wash away the stains and wounds that we have so cleverly hidden from everyone except God. He has known about them all along, and He has wanted to set us free. Finally, we must allow Him to deliver us by working with Him, not against Him. It is all because of the shed Blood of our beloved Lord Jesus Christ.

Let me just say this, being called a Christian does not make us Christians. The name does not mean anything if we are not exemplifying the Lord and His nature. Wearing a cross does not make us Christians. I have seen some pretty shady characters with a big, gold cross around their necks who looked at me with scorn when I said to them, "Oh, you're a Christian?" Nope, they were just wearing a cross.

Let me share an incident that makes my point quite well. I was talking to a woman who worked at a local hospital. I happened to mention that one of my members worked in her department. I began to describe the woman's physical characteristics to her. I went on, "She's so nice. Active in church services, she's one of the sweetest ladies." This woman looked at me kind of stunned. "I know a woman with that name who looks like the person you are describing, but I don't know the woman you're talking about. The woman who works in my department has a foul mouth and a sharp tongue. As a matter of fact, nobody wants to have anything to do with her. I think, perhaps, we are speaking about two different people." The sad thing was, we weren't. We were actually talking about the same person. She acted one way in church, and another way at work.

We have to grab hold of these truths and really make a change, my friend. The world needs what Jesus has provided, but *we* have to get it first. I know I have been redundant over many topics in this book. I have purposely stated the same things in as many different ways as I can think of. We must get this. This is the answer for the hurting and the wounded. Though forgiven, we have been as dirty and common as the world because of past sins. No wonder we have not been able to really impress anyone with our Christianity. But things can change, and they can change dramatically. There is hope for our hearts. Thank God. I want to plant in your soul a hope—an exceeding great hope—a hope that cannot easily be quenched. Grab hold, let it grow, and do not turn loose of it in the name of Jesus Christ, our Lord!

WHAT KIND OF CHRISTIAN?

The devil will be the first one to tell us that the Blood does not and will not work to cleanse and heal. He whispers things like, "How many times have you already prayed? How many tears have you cried...and nothing has changed. What kind of a Christian are you anyway? You are still doing the same dumb things."

So we go to the altar again at church and cry until we "feel" better. We thank God, walk out of the church talking to ourselves about how we are going to do better...how we are going to get a handle on things...how we are going to make this thing work. Do you understand? That is works—what *we* are going to do in our own power—not grace. Our flesh will always fail us. We cannot rely on it or our good intentions; it is not a matter of us trying harder. I've tried so hard it is just downright pitiful. I've tried endless times, but it did not get the job done. I was still a mess. See, it is not a matter of us, it is a matter of *Him* and what He has done for us. Without a doubt, that is a different ball game. In Him we can win every time.

Without fail, believers want to be vessels of honor for God and uplift the name of Jesus with our lifestyle and conversation. True born-again Christians do not want to be hypocrites—people who say one thing and do another and do not walk what they preach. Many times I have heard people say, "I'm not going to church. They are just a bunch of hypocrites there." Occasionally, they are right. We say "Love, love, love," but treat everyone around us unkindly. We act real spiritual, but have not opened our Bible in months. Help us, Jesus.

People act like hypocrites sometimes because they are not acting like true Christians. This is because they do not know who they are in Christ Jesus. They do not know or understand what He accomplished for them on the Cross. Nor do they know their rights and privileges in Christ, or how to apply the Blood of Jesus and let Him take care of their sin nature. Not knowing these things is against what our born-again spirit desires, I assure you.

The more I apply the Blood to my heart, the more disturbing it is to me when I find myself not walking in the things of God, so I continue to faithfully apply the Blood. To be quite honest, the power of the Blood of Jesus holds our greatest hope for ever being conformed to the image of the Lord Jesus. Depending on how deceitful our hearts are, it may take a while to see results—but hang in there. Do not stop. We will eventually begin to experience a softening of our hearts, a desire to know God in a much deeper way and to serve Him. The Blood of Jesus will soften our hardened hearts so we can be tender toward Him and His desires for us and others.

RELEASE FAITH

Release your faith and begin speaking every day: "Thank You, Father, that my heart is being softened. Thank You that my old evil heart of unbelief is being transformed by the Blood of the Morning and Evening Sacrifice. Thank You for changing my heart so that it is tender toward You. Glory to God! Please wash me, cleanse me, rearrange me, change me. My heart longs and hungers for the things of God. I will see into Your Kingdom—my eyes do see and my ears do hear. The voice of strangers I will not follow. Because of the change You are making in my heart, I have the mind of Christ, and I will obey Your voice quickly. Out of my mouth like a fountain come words of life to others who are hurting."

When we confess these types of things, we may not immediately begin to release our faith because sometimes we simply do not believe those confessions yet, but we will if we keep saying them. We need to speak what we desire (see Mark 11:23-34).

Looking for the blessed hope and glorious appearing of our great God and Savior Jesus Christ, who gave Himself for us, that He might redeem us from every lawless deed and purify for Himself His own special people, zealous for good works (Tit. 2:13-14).

This Scripture in Titus 2 speaks of being zealous for the things of God. When we realize the sin nature has been resolved and conquered, we will be zealous for the things of God. What does that mean? It means we will want to serve God and will be hungry for the things of God. Our heart's cry will be, "I want to be in Your Word. I need to know Your Word and Your heart, dear Jesus." These things of God bring life and hope to us. How many have taken their lives because they thought they had no hope of escaping their problems or sins? Too many. I am sorry to say too many did not hear the Good News in time. I want to shout it from the housetops, *"The Blood is bigger and greater than any problem!"*

Even though at times it may seem impossible, there is no impossible situation when we get God involved! When we try to hide sins instead of facing and dealing with them head-on, the pressure gets worse. Guilt and shame rise up in fury. We do not want to do that thing, but we have not been able to conquer it. We become afraid that we will be judged because we cannot turn it loose. Yes, regrettably some will judge. Funny thing is, even though they have their own problems that they are dealing with, they will always have something to say about our failure.

The devil will use anything to destroy us, anything at all. But our eternal destination is based on our belief in and receipt of God's salvation.

CHAPTER 11

STANDING IN CONFIDENCE

Seeing then that we have a great High Priest who has passed through the heavens, Jesus the Son of God, let us hold fast our confession. For we do not have a High Priest who cannot sympathize with our weaknesses, but was in all points tempted as we are, yet without sin (Hebrews 4:14-15).

Thank God we have a High Priest who can help us. It's fabulous to know that we are not in this world as orphans, floundering without assistance. We have help in high places! Praise God forevermore. We have been living far beneath our privileges, but Jesus is there to help us. He is there to lift us up and give us victory over every problem that we face! Glory to God!

> But **Christ came as High Priest** *of the* **good things** *to come, with the greater and more perfect tabernacle not made with hands, that is, not of this creation. Not with the blood of goats and calves, but* **with His own blood He entered the Most Holy Place once for all**, *having obtained eternal redemption. For if the blood of bulls and goats and the ashes of a heifer, sprinkling the unclean, sanctifies for the purifying of the flesh, how much more shall the blood of Christ, who through the eternal Spirit offered Himself without spot to God, cleanse your conscience from dead works to serve the living God?* (Hebrews 9:11-14)

The people were looking for Messiah. They were looking for somebody to come and set up God's Kingdom. The word *Christ* means "Messiah, the Anointed One." So here in verse 11 there is an acknowledgment that the Messiah has come. He came as the High Priest of good things to come. He did not come with bad things, but good things; and you and I need to find out what those good things are. At the top of the list is the Blood He poured out, not only at Calvary, but on the heavenly Mercy Seat! That Blood brings forth good things. Hallelujah.

In verse 14, the word *conscience* means "the thoughts and attitudes of the heart." We all have problems with our thoughts and attitudes from time to time. So this Scripture passage says that the Blood of Jesus can purge our thoughts and attitudes. It can totally cleanse our wicked hearts (soulish area), our deceived *and deceiving* hearts. The Blood can purge our hearts of dead works so that we can serve the living God. The Blood can change the way we think if we apply it to our hearts! We can go free if we give Him something to work with and then let Him do it!

But this Scripture passage also says to me that if our conscience is not purged, we cannot serve God. If our thoughts and attitudes have not been changed, we are restrained from fully serving Him. Friend, this is serious business, isn't it? We are not little islands unto ourselves or little flies on the wall going through life. We are here with destiny in our blood—His Blood flowing through our veins. We must think His thoughts, and thank God, He has given us a way to do that.

Jesus fulfilled the law for us. We are not under the letter of the law, but under the law of the Spirit of life in Christ Jesus. He has set us free and paid the ransom; we have been redeemed, justified, and made righteous by His blood.

> *Therefore do not cast away your confidence, which has great reward. For you have need of endurance, so that after you have done the will of God, you may receive the promise: "For yet a little while, and He who is coming will come and will not tarry. Now the just shall live by faith; but if anyone draws back, My soul has no pleasure in him." But we are not of those who draw back to perdition, but of those who believe to the saving of the soul* (Hebrews 10:35-39).

This passage of Scripture in Hebrews 10 is along the same lines. If our thoughts and attitudes are not purged by the Blood, then we will cast away our confidence and we will not be able to stand. We will draw back unless our hearts are cleansed. We have to believe in the saving of our soul, by faith, for the just live by faith. By faith, we believe what the Blood will do for us, that it will cleanse our thought patterns so they will line up with the will of God, the ways of God, and enable us to stand strong without drawing back from Him. That is only done by faith in the Word of God.

> *Therefore not even the first covenant was dedicated without blood. For when Moses had spoken every precept to all the people according to the law, he took the blood of calves and goats, with water, scarlet wool, and hyssop, and sprinkled both the book itself and all the people, saying, "This is the blood of the covenant which God has commanded you." Then likewise he sprinkled with blood both the tabernacle and all the vessels of the ministry* (Hebrews 9:18-21).

We are comparing what Jesus did with what Moses did because, remember, Jesus fulfilled the Old Covenant. So what Moses did in the natural, Jesus did in the Spirit dimension. The Bible says that Moses sprinkled the book with blood. That would be the book of the law that they carried with them. It also says Moses sprinkled all of the people to cleanse them. "Vessels of ministry" is a key phrase, because in the spirit realm, we are the vessels of ministry. Let's take a look at another Scripture:

> *Nevertheless the solid foundation of God stands, having this seal: "The Lord knows those who are His," and, "Let everyone who names the name of Christ **depart from iniquity**." But in a great house there are not only vessels of gold and silver, but also of wood and clay, some for honor and some for dishonor. Therefore if anyone **cleanses** himself from the latter, he will be a vessel for honor, sanctified and useful for the Master, prepared for every good work* (2 Timothy 2:19-21).

We are the vessels of ministry, but it says we have to purge, cleanse ourselves of sin and its residue with the Blood to prepare us as vessels of honor. If we do not apply the power of the Blood and go through a cleansing of our hearts, even though we are vessels of ministry, we will be one of dishonor. And that choice is completely up to us. Almighty God has given us the key to move from dishonor to honor by purging ourselves with the Blood of Jesus. Working with God, our hearts can be cleansed so we can serve Him honorably. That's glorious news. How exciting our lives *can* change. There is hope for our hearts. Praise God.

> *And according to the law almost all things are purified with blood, and without shedding of blood there is no remission. Therefore it was necessary that the*

copies of the things in the heavens should be purified with these, but the heavenly things themselves with better sacrifices than these (Hebrews 9:22-23).

Many think we can act like the devil and God will open up His arms and say, "Come on in," when it cost the Blood of His Son Jesus to purchase us. This is a serious matter.

And you, being dead in your trespasses and the uncircumcision of your flesh, He has made alive together with Him, having forgiven you all trespasses, having wiped out the handwriting of requirements that was against us, which was contrary to us. And He has taken it out of the way, having nailed it to the cross (Colossians 2:13-14).

But look what He did: God not only forgave our sin, made us alive in Him, and raised us up to be with Him, He also blotted out the handwriting of all the bad things that were written against us. There is no record of it anymore in Heaven. His Blood has wiped it clean. In other words, the Bible tells us that He made it so that we could start a life of faith with a clean slate. Our sins, though they are many, can be washed away that we may be as white as snow. In God's eyes, the residue of those former sins does not exist.

Apply the Blood, dear one, and walk free. Do not be tormented another day, not one more hour. The precious Blood of Jesus has taken care of our sins and iniquities and wiped away our yesterdays. God nailed it all to the Cross, and it died there that we could be made new.

Hallelujah!

CHAPTER 12

FREE AT LAST!

The Cross of Calvary went to the root of our sin-stained life and totally destroyed it! But are we allowing the Blood to work throughout every aspect of our lives? I doubt it. Until we can grab hold of this truth and embrace it, our freedom from shame and guilt will continue to elude us.

We need to say, "No, no more. Sin, you no longer have power over me. You are a snake whose head has been cut off by the power of Almighty God! You are over there wiggling, acting like you are still alive and have control over me, but you are headless. Jesus is my Lord. Neither sin nor iniquity will control me anymore.

It takes courage to say those kinds of things and to make those types of declarations, especially if we continue to mess up. But that is what faith is—believing something we cannot see, and *seeing* in our spirit the things that are not yet manifested. When we keep doing the same dumb thing over and over again—whether it is losing our temper, having a bad attitude, or speaking with a sharp tongue—it is terribly harmful. We have to break out of the rut, which takes courage and faith in God and His glorious Word.

Faith is built on what we know. We use the term *blind faith,* but there is no such thing. Faith sees the end result based entirely on God's Word—the Holy Bible. God is not a man who lies (Num. 23:19). Trust Him. Let's build our faith on that Word by hearing it over and over again, and talk to ourselves saying, "My God took care of this sin. He also took care of the root of it. No, I am not going to spend the rest of my life acting like this. I am not going around this mountain forty times." Once that Word—a *rhema* word— becomes a living part of us, our trips around the mountain will cease. Revelation can come quickly or it can be long and tedious depending on our decisions and how much time and attention we give the Word of God.

We know that *"by His stripes we are the healed"* (Isa. 53:5); we are not the sick. Glory to God! Before getting that revelation, though, we all go around the mountain many times. That mountain of sickness is so well traveled that there is a rut there, a beaten path that holds us from breaking free. We have a lot of company going around that mountain, including family and friends. Think of how much time is spent conversing with each other about "our" sicknesses and tending our sicknesses. No, Scripture says He *"bore our sicknesses"* (Matt. 8:17; see also Isa. 53:3-5;

1 Pet. 2:24). Whatever sickness or disease is on us cannot be ours, because *"He took our sicknesses and removed our diseases"* (Matt. 8:17 NLT).

We are so good at going around the mountain, we can go around blindfolded, on one leg, even. Did you know that a lot of people refuse to hear the great truth about healing? They do not want to get out of the rut, even when they can go free from sickness and disease. It is just too hard for them. Perhaps they are ridiculed by their family members, and they back off. Remember, many times when we decide to believe God, the "religious" people will not be happy.

MAKING THE MOVE

Let's think about Peter walking on the water (see Matt. 14:22-32). The Lord said, "Come." He did not say, "Peter, come!" But Peter was the one who decided to step out and go to Him. All the other disciples probably said, "Peter, don't act foolish, get back in the boat. You're going to get in trouble out on the water. People can't walk on water!" Jesus did not limit that experience to just Peter. They all could have stepped out of the boat and experienced the miraculous, but they did not. Only Peter made the move.

But remember, Peter did not walk on the water, he walked on the Word of God, "Come." If we think everybody is going to be happy because we decide to go free by trusting God, we are mistaken. Surely you do not think the others in the boat said, "Oh, praise God, Peter, we're with you! Get in the water.

We're with you, brother. You can do it! Go for it." Are you kidding? If they were saying that, they would have stepped out of the boat with him. No, Peter was on his own, and so are we sometimes when it is just God's marvelous Word and us. And in truth, that is all we really need—just a Word from God.

Scripture states that the road leading to destruction is broad and there are many who are traveling it, but narrow is the one leading to everlasting life and few are they who find that path (see Matt. 7:13-14). Isn't that the same principle as the one I have been teaching throughout this book? Hell is a real option, but we do not have to go there. Sickness is real, but we do not have to accept it. We often miss the mark and sin, but sin does not have to control us. The wonderful news is that we can walk away from all of that mess and live a glorious life, always submissive to God and believing His Word with all of our hearts.

Then why are people going to hell when Jesus does not want them to go there? Because they do not know or believe the provision that Jesus has shed His Blood to redeem them from it. Why aren't we walking in victory over sin when the price has been paid to redeem us from it? Why do we let sin and shame rule and reign over us when Jesus is supposedly our King? Why do we bow our knee to things that we have already been redeemed from? We have all done it, at least in days past. We either do not know, or we do not believe what we do know enough to act on it. It is that simple.

I do not understand how He accomplished such an extraordinary freedom for us. It is miraculous; I do not even have the words to express how marvelous it is. But one thing I *do* know—*greater is He who is in us than he who is in the world!* (1 John 4:4). And our God does not lie! What God did, He did completely—and He did it for you and me because He loves us.

Things somehow change down in the deep places of our hearts when we receive revelation that sin has lost its power over us. How long the sin and its wounds and defilements linger depends upon how long we will allow it to do so. If we just put up with it, then we will keep it.

At times, it is like we think we have to twist God's arm to do something for us. We are so wrong. Our God is so loving, so kind, and so wonderful. He really does want us to be free, and we can walk in that freedom. We can stand firm and continue against all odds to proclaim our freedom—even though we are not acting free—and know the Blood is working on our behalf. There is no stronger power on this earth than the precious Blood of our Savior, the Lord Jesus Christ. It is Him and Him alone. He is the *only* Savior. With all that He has done, how could we not love Him? How could we not be forever grateful for His mercy and grace? Believe in the power of the Blood of the Lamb. To His honor and glory, you will walk free!

> *Wash me thoroughly from mine iniquity, and cleanse me from my sin. Purge me with hyssop, and I shall be clean: wash me, and I shall be whiter than snow.*

Create in me a clean heart, O God; and renew a right spirit within me (Psalm 51:2,7,10)

CHAPTER 13

THE HEALING POWER OF THE BLOOD

I have explained in the previous chapters about the power of the Blood to cleanse us from sin and reconcile us to God, which is *great* news. Well, I have more great news! The Blood can bring healing! The Bible teaches that forgiveness of sins and healing for the body go together. They cannot be separated. The following truths from the Bible will help convince you of that.

- King David, in Psalm 103, listed the various benefits of redemption, and he lists forgiveness of sins and healing of diseases first. They are the main benefits of redemption. Forgiveness and healing are listed together, side by side, in the same verse because the two go together. "Bless the Lord, O my soul; and all that is within me, bless His holy name! Bless the Lord,

O my soul, and forget not all His benefits: who **forgives all your iniquities**, who **heals all your diseases**" (Ps. 103:1-3).

- When Jesus was ministering, a paralyzed man was brought to Him for healing. Jesus said to him, "Son, your sins are forgiven you" (Mark 2:5). The man did not come looking for forgiveness of his sins; he came looking for healing. Jesus looked at the scribes who were questioning His right to forgive sins and said to them, "Which is easier, to say to the paralytic, 'Your sins are forgiven you,' or to say, 'Arise, take up your bed and walk'? But that you may know that the Son of Man has power on earth to forgive sins"—He said to the paralytic, "I say to you, arise, take up your bed, and go to your house" (Mark 2:9-11). And the paralyzed man did just that. Jesus was making a statement about who He was. He was saying in essence, "The work I came to do will take care of sins and take care of sickness too." Forgiveness of sins and healing of diseases go together. As I've said many times, it's "six of one, half a dozen of the other." Both forgiveness and healing were part of the ministry of Jesus, and both were part of His atoning work of Calvary. You cannot separate the two.

- Isaiah 53:5 tells us that by the stripes (wounds) of Jesus we are healed. The word "healed" in this verse is translated from the Hebrew word rapha, which means "healed, cured, mended, repaired, physician." I am providing you the definition so you will know the word "healed" in this verse is speaking of physical healing, not spiritual healing. That means the beating He endured provided for our physical healing. The price Jesus paid for our sins to be forgiven (we call it atonement) was death by crucifixion. On the way to the Cross, He was tied to a whipping post and beaten. The beating—the provision for our healing—was part of the whole atonement process. You cannot separate the two.

- Sickness came into the world as a result of sin. I have already established that we have been redeemed from sin. If we are redeemed from sin, then we are redeemed from the effects of sin, and that includes sickness! You cannot separate the two.

- The Blood of Jesus provided for the forgiveness of our sins. How was His Blood shed? Through His wounds. Because of the Blood, through His wounds, we have forgiveness of sins. Because of the Blood, through His wounds, we have healing for our bodies. You cannot separate the two.

Forgiveness is provided through the Blood, and healing is provided through the Blood! We have been forgiven, and we have been made whole—spirit, soul, *and body*—because of the Blood of Jesus. Glory to His name!

We have to settle it in our hearts that it *is* God's will for us to be healed. The Bible tells us Jesus came to destroy the works of the devil (1 John 3:8). The Blood of Jesus is the power that destroyed the works of the devil. It all began when Adam and Eve fell for the deception of the enemy and ate the forbidden fruit. Sin was born and the great fall of man took place (Gen. 2:16-17). At that time, spiritual death entered the earth. Spiritual death led to physical death. There was no sickness, disease, or death until sin entered the world. Therefore, since sin was a result of the work of the enemy, so was disease. There would be but one remedy for sin—the Blood of Jesus. That same Blood would be the remedy to remove sickness.

Jesus says in John 10:10-11,14:

> *The thief does not come except to steal, and to kill, and to destroy. I have come that they may have life, and that they may have it more abundantly. I am the good shepherd. The good shepherd gives His life for the sheep. ...I am the good shepherd; and I know My sheep, and am known by My own.*

Jesus was giving His Word that He would be the sacrifice to purchase man's redemption from sin and sickness. There was a price to be paid. God had been wronged through the sinful behavior of the first two humans. In order for man to once again have fellowship with the Father, there had to be a price paid for redemption and reconciliation. Jesus was the price, the ransom. *This precious gift of salvation includes healing for our bodies.*

You may have thought to yourself, *Well, I don't know if it's God's will for me to be healed.* Think about it this way: if it were not the Father's will for sick people to be made well, would His Son have been healing every sick person who came to Him for healing?! No, He wouldn't. But He did! And let's remind ourselves…the Bible tells us Jesus did *only* what the Father showed Him to do (John 5:19).

God wants you to be healed just like He wants you to be saved. How do we know that? By the authority of His Word. Go look in the Bible. Find out what God says about His will, His desire to heal you. Go ahead, look it up. His Word says:

> *He sent His word and healed them, and delivered them from their destructions* (Psalm 107:20).

> *For they [His words] are life to those who find them, and health to all their flesh* (Proverbs 4:22).

> *Bless the Lord, O my soul, and forget not all His benefits: who forgives all your iniquities, who heals all your diseases* (Psalm 103:2-3).

"MY BLOOD TOOK CARE OF THAT"

Some years ago, I was talking to the Lord about healing. He said to me, "Name one reason why I will not heal you."

I began to name this reason and that reason, things related to the past. He said, "But My Blood took care of that." And then I gave Him reasons people have given me over the years about why they think God won't heal them, things that have caused them to feel guilty or unworthy. Every time I named something, He said, "But My Blood took care of that."

And then I thought of things in the present, things that may be a hindrance in my walk with Him. He said, "Ask Me to forgive you, and My Blood will take care of that." Then I would think of something else and begin to say it and I'd hear Him say, "But My Blood took care of that." I could not name one thing that He did not respond with, "But My Blood took care of that." It was so freeing to hear the Lord say that to me! What a wonderful, merciful God we serve!

Can you think of one reason God would not heal you? Whatever it is, His Blood took care of that. There is absolutely no reason why you should not expect God to heal you. Whatever may come up before the Father—our actions or deeds, an accusation by the enemy, a sin or sickness—Jesus can respond, "BUT MY BLOOD TOOK CARE OF THAT." It is all about the Blood, the precious, cleansing, healing Blood of Jesus. Jesus truly is our sin-bearer and He is our sickness-bearer. The following Scriptures attest to that:

> *Surely He has borne our griefs and carried our sorrows; yet we esteemed Him stricken, smitten by God, and afflicted. But **He was wounded for our transgressions**, He was **bruised for our iniquities**;*

the chastisement for our peace was upon Him, and
by His stripes we are healed (Isaiah 53:4-5).

That it might be fulfilled which was spoken by
*Isaiah the prophet, saying: "**He Himself took our***
***infirmities, and bore our sicknesses**" (Matthew*
8:17).

*Who **Himself bore our sins in His own body** on*
the tree, that we, having died to sins, might live for
*righteousness—**by whose stripes you were healed***
(1 Peter 2:24).

Let's take God at His Word and believe for our healing
through the Blood of Jesus!

HE CAN AND WILL

In Matthew 8:2-3, a leper came to Jesus and said, *"Lord, if You*
are willing, You can make me clean." This is an age-old question that many are still wondering about today: "I know God
can heal me, but *will* He heal me?" This Scripture forever set-
tles that question. When Jesus said, "I will," He was not just
saying, "Ok, I'll do it." The Greek word translated *will* actually means "to intend, to desire, to take delight in." It is His
delight for us to be well—free of sickness, disease, and pain.

The Father's intent is for us to be made whole, and Jesus'
finished work at the Cross accomplished that. One of the
reasons I love this passage in Matthew 8 is because it shows
the marvelous compassion of Jesus. The leper was considered "untouchable." But Jesus did not hesitate to touch him.

No one is untouchable in the eyes of Jesus. He touched him and cleansed him and made him whole. It was His delight to do so.

How do we know healing is for today? There are those who say, "Yes, Jesus healed. And yes, the apostles healed. But all of that passed away with the last apostle." How absurd! Jesus healed people Himself, and He healed people through the apostles, and He has healed multitudes down through the ages. I have received His healing numerous times. And I have seen thousands healed by Him. *His desire for people to be made well has never changed.* The Bible tells us that *"Jesus Christ is the same yesterday, today, and forever"* (Heb. 13:8). He has not changed. And He never will.

THE DETOUR

I have already spoken of the horrible, tortuous beating Jesus endured. Have you ever thought about this? Jesus could have been born, grown up, entered into ministry for three years, then gone straight to the Cross where He would die as the Lamb of God, paying the price for our redemption. His death and the pouring out of His Blood would put us in right standing with the Father, give us a home in Heaven, and place us into relationship with Him so we can experience His presence and His love. All of that would have been accomplished by the Cross.

So why did Jesus take that detour on the way to the Cross and give Himself over to the whipping post? There is only one reason: so our bodies could be made whole! I am so thankful He made the provision for our healing as part of the atonement!

I have already mentioned the Hebrew word *rapha*, which means "healing." But did you know that word is in one of God's names? One of His names is Jehovah Rapha, which means "the Lord who heals." Did you get what I just said? Healing is His name! The names of God are a reflection of His character and His nature. Healing is His name! It is His nature to bring healing! It is His nature to bring wholeness! How could we ever question God's willingness to heal?

Let's get one more thing straight. God does not put sickness on us! The enemy does. Jesus suffered terribly to pay the high price for our bodies to be healed and made whole. He did that because He and the Father desire that we be well. If He went through that horrible, torturous beating in order to provide healing for us, why would God then turn around and put sickness on us? To do so would make a mockery of the pain and suffering His Son endured.

God does not punish us with sickness. I do not know whether you have children or not, but if you do, I know one thing for certain: you have no desire to see any terrible disease come upon them. Even when you get angry or upset or disappointed with them, you have no desire to see them sick or in pain. You would never want illness to come upon them as a punishment or to teach them a lesson.

God is a far better, more loving parent than any of us could ever be. Our heavenly Father's love is perfect and pure, not tainted by sin and the effects of a fallen world. He wants only good things for His children. His desire is to see you healthy and whole.

COMPLETE WHOLENESS

Perhaps you are still questioning the power of the Blood to deal with physical illness. Perhaps you believe the Blood only cleanses your spirit from sin and heals your soul from mental and emotional torments. Let the Scriptures reveal the truth to you. The Word of God gives clear revelation concerning all that Jesus accomplished for us as the sacrificial Lamb. Isaiah 53:4 tells us, *"He has borne our griefs and carried our sorrows."* The Hebrew word translated *griefs* means "sickness," and the word *sorrows* means "pains." So we could read it this way: *He bore our sickness and carried our pains.* What a revelation! We do not have to live with pain in our bodies! We do not have to live with disease! Glory to God! Jesus, through His death and resurrection, provided wholeness for our spirit, soul, *and* body.

Isaiah also speaks of this wholeness when he says the *"chastisement of our peace was upon Him"* (Is. 53:5). In other words, the punishment for us to obtain peace was upon Jesus. The word translated "peace" is the Hebrew word *shalom. Shalom* is a wonderful Hebrew word that means wholeness and completeness. It carries the connotation of "nothing missing, nothing broken, nothing lacking." The word *shalom* reflects God's desire for us—wholeness in every area of our lives!

Romans 10:10 tells us, *"For with the heart one believes unto righteousness, and with the mouth confession is made unto salvation."* However, this Scripture is speaking about far more than just forgiveness of sins. The word translated "salvation" has a greater meaning than is generally taught. This Greek word is *sozo,* which is an all-encompassing word. It means "salvation, healing, deliverance, wholeness, protection, and preservation." All of that is included in our salvation. The Blood of Jesus gives us full access to *sozo.*

Psalm 145:8 tells us the Lord is gracious and full of compassion and of great mercy. He yearns for us to be well, to walk in the healing and wholeness He has provided for us. We see in the Scriptures over and over that Jesus was moved with compassion to help and to heal. That is who He is. He is filled with mercy and compassion for you. He desires to see you well, walking in all the benefits of redemption. He wants good things for you and *only* good things. Believe that because He loves you and has mercy and compassion toward you, He will see you through every trial, every affliction.

God loves us with a great, incomprehensible love. He desires that we prosper and be in good health (3 John 1:2). He made the provision for us to walk in the fullness of His love and blessings through His Blood. God has given us all things that pertain to life (2 Pet. 1:3-4). He made provisions for us to have *zoe* life, which is the Greek word that means the "God kind of life"—a real life, active, vigorous, and blessed. The kind of life only God can give.

BELIEVE

As I taught in my book *The Simplicity of Healing,* our ability to walk in healing has been made simple. Jesus did all the hard work for us. All we have to do is simply *believe* that by His stripes we are healed. We simply *believe* He already bore our sickness and bore our pain in His own body, and therefore we do not have to bear it in ours! Because we believe, we speak what we believe. We say, "By His stripes, I am healed!" We speak it in faith. It's that simple. We believe it. And we speak it.

Now that does not mean that sickness will never come upon us. We have sickness because we have an enemy. He is the one who brings illness. He is hoping you do not know that Jesus made the provision for your healing, hoping you do not know that disease has no right to be on you, hoping you do not know the Word of God—and even if you do, he is hoping you will not stand on God's Word. He is hoping you will just receive the illness and succumb to it.

But you are *not* going to receive it, and you are *not* going to succumb to it! You now know you have been redeemed from sickness! You can say, "LORD, I THANK YOU THAT YOU ALREADY BORE THIS DISEASE IN YOUR OWN BODY, AND I DO NOT HAVE TO BEAR IT IN MINE! LORD, I THANK YOU THAT BY YOUR STRIPES I AM HEALED!"

When we speak those words, we are speaking about the power of the Blood. The Blood brings healing! There is no more powerful substance in the universe! So believe, speak, and be healed!

I hope you are convinced of the goodness of your God and of His desire for you to be well and whole. He loves you so very much. It is His delight for you to be free of the guilt of sin. It is His delight for you to be free of sickness and pain. Jesus came into this world so He could set you free from sin *and* sickness, and He shed His very own Blood so you could walk in that freedom.

Be free! For God so loved you that He shed His Blood for you. God so loved you that He provided salvation for your spirit, peace for your soul, and healing for your body. Thank God for the cleansing, healing power of the Blood!

BECAUSE OF THE BLOOD...

I am clean.

> *But if we walk in the light as He is in the light, we have fellowship with one another, and the blood of Jesus Christ His Son cleanses us from all sin* (1 John 1:7).

I am purified.

> *...To Him who loved us and washed us from our sins in His own blood* (Revelation 1:5).

I am forgiven.

> *In Him we have redemption through His blood, the forgiveness of sins, according to the riches of His grace* (Ephesians 1:7).

I am healed and at peace.

> *But He was wounded for our transgressions, He was bruised for our iniquities; the chastisement for*

our peace was upon Him, and by His stripes we are healed (Isaiah 53:5).

I have been made righteous.

For He made Him who knew no sin to be sin for us, that we might become the righteousness of God in Him (2 Corinthians 5:21).

I have been justified.

Being justified freely by His grace through the redemption that is in Christ Jesus, whom God set forth as a propitiation by His blood, through faith, to demonstrate His righteousness, because in His forbearance God had passed over the sins that were previously committed (Romans 3:24-25).

I am free from the fear of wrath.

Much more then, having now been justified by His blood, we shall be saved from wrath through Him (Romans 5:9).

I've been brought near to God.

But now in Christ Jesus you who once were far off have been brought near by the blood of Christ (Ephesians 2:13).

I have the power to overcome the enemy.

And they overcame him by the blood of the Lamb and by the word of their testimony, and they did not love their lives to the death (Revelation 12:11).

I am redeemed from the curse.

Christ has redeemed us from the curse of the law, having become a curse for us, for it is written, "Cursed is everyone who hangs on a tree" (Galatians 3:13).

I am free from a guilty conscience.

Therefore, brethren, having boldness to enter the Holiest by the blood of Jesus, by a new and living way which He consecrated for us, through the veil, that is, His flesh, and having a High Priest over the house of God, let us draw near with a true heart in full assurance of faith, having our hearts sprinkled from an evil conscience and our bodies washed with pure water (Hebrews 10:19-22).

I have revelation of my Heavenly Father through Jesus.

Who being the brightness of His glory and the express image of His person, and upholding all things by the word of His power, when He had by Himself purged our sins, sat down at the right hand of the Majesty on high (Hebrews 1:3).

I am redeemed by something more precious than silver or gold.

Knowing that you were not redeemed with corruptible things, like silver or gold, from your aimless conduct received by tradition from your fathers, but with the precious blood of Christ, as of a lamb without blemish and without spot (1 Peter 1:18-19).

I can partake of the sweet communion of remembrance.

And He took bread, gave thanks and broke it, and gave it to them, saying, "This is My body which is given for you; do this in remembrance of Me." Likewise He also took the cup after supper, saying, "This cup is the new covenant in My blood, which is shed for you (Luke 22:19-20).

Dear heavenly Father,

I thank You for the Cross of Calvary and the precious Blood of Jesus. I thank You that because of the Blood, I am forgiven, cleansed, healed, and made whole. I'm no longer hindered in my walk with You because of guilt or condemnation or past mistakes. I can now walk free, able to draw near and enjoy my relationship with You as never before.

I ask You to lead and guide me on the path of life and enable me to fulfill the high calling You have for me. I can rest assured that because of the Blood of Jesus, You will help me, protect me, and provide for me. Through the power of the Blood I will fulfill my God-given purpose and show forth your goodness and your glory.

In Jesus' name. Amen.

ABOUT THE AUTHOR

As a young child growing up on a farm in Midville, Georgia, Dr. Sandra Kennedy recognized the call of God upon her life. She felt His compassion for people to be healed and delivered through the power of His marvelous Word.

Dr. Kennedy founded Whole Life Ministries in Augusta, Georgia, in 1983 as a result of a vision given her by the Lord. Whole Life Ministries is a nondenominational, multicultural church dedicated to lifting up the name of Jesus Christ and changing lives through the power of God's Word. In that same vision, the Lord gave her the mandate to "grow up the Body of Christ and teach them victory."

In addition to pastoring, Dr. Kennedy produces television and internet programs and is a sought-after conference speaker. She also founded The Healing Teams Ministry and The Healing Center at Whole Life Ministries, and oversees a number of other community outreach programs. She has had the privilege of teaching and preaching throughout the United States and in many nations around the world.

Dr. Kennedy loves to teach the Word of God in all its fullness and has a special passion for teaching the power of God's Word to bring healing and wholeness to people's lives. She has seen thousands healed and set free from every kind of bondage.

Dr. Kennedy is a woman of integrity who is motivated by a spirit of excellence. Her heart's desire is to see God's plans and purposes fulfilled in the earth, and she inspires others to pursue godliness. The driving force behind all that she does is a genuine love for people and a strong desire to see them saved, healed, and delivered.

FREE E-BOOKS?
YES, PLEASE!

Get **FREE** and deeply discounted **Christian books** for your **e-reader** delivered to your inbox **every week!**

IT'S SIMPLE!

VISIT lovetoreadclub.com

SUBSCRIBE by entering your email address

RECEIVE free and discounted e-book offers and inspiring articles delivered to your inbox every week!

Unsubscribe at any time.

SUBSCRIBE NOW!

> ## LOVE TO READ CLUB

visit **LOVETOREADCLUB.COM** ▶